Dancing on Sand

Images
Word Pictures
Poetry
Fragmented Moments

John S Litchen

All rights reserved. No part of this publication may be reproduced by any means including photocopying or other information storage and retrieval systems without written consent of the publisher and author except for small portions which may be quoted for the purpose of reviewing the work as a whole. The right of John Litchen to be identified as the author of this work has been asserted by him in accordance with the Copyright, Design and Patents Act 1988.

ISBN: 978-0-6459983-0-6
Copyright © J S Litchen 2024

Published by Yambu
3 Firestone Court
Robina, Qld 4226.

jlitchen@bigpond.net.au

Dancing on Sand

Images
Word Pictures
Poetry
Fragmented Moments

John S Litchen

Yambu

John Litchen

Para Monica

siempre en mi corazon

Table of Contents

- page- 7 - Dancing on Sand, Bailando en la arena
- page - 8 - Mi Camino
- page- 9 - Canola
- page- 10 - La Luz Tremenda, The Terrible Light
- page- 11- La Sombra de la Muerte. The Shadow of death
- page- 12- Pensamientos, - Thoughts
- page- 15- Another Onslaught
- page- 20- Homecoming
- page- 22- Talk to me
- page- 24- Llorando
- page- 26- Some Thoughts
- page- 29- Leaving Iquique
- page- 37- Refuge
- page- 42- Flores
- page- 43- Birds in our Garden (photos)
- page- 50- A duck in the Pool
- page- 64- Noises in the Night
- page- 68- Sands of Time
- page- 70- Sand in an Hourglass
- page- 71- Questions
- page- 76- The Gellibrand Pile Light
- page- 79- The Gift of Sight
- page- 80- En La Playa
- page- 84- Empty Eyes
- page- 85- The Path into Darkness
- page- 97- A view of apocalypse
- page- 104- Momentos efimeros - Ephemeral moments
- page- 105- A conversation on a summer's day
- page- 106- A pesar de todo
- page- 107- Despite everything
- page- 110- Algo indisputable
- page- 111- Something indisputable
- page- 112- Addendum

On a cold winter's day on the beach at Cape Schank in 1969, Christine and Zara were tap-dancing on hard sand in an attempt to keep warm.

"I can tap-dance too," Phillip said, and proceeded to show them his tap dancing skills.

Bailando en la arena

Bailando en la arena
deja pisos efímeros
mudados por vientos.
Limpiados por las mareas
lo que deja de nuestro baile
es la playa inviolable
hasta al fin del mundo.

Dancing on Sand

Dancing on sand
leaves ephemeral footprints
erased by shifting wind.
Cleansed by tides
the remains of our dance
is the beach inviolate
'till the end of time.

Mi camino

Con felicidad, cantando.
En mi camino de la vida,
ando bailando.

Portarlington, December 1977, in a field of canola.

Canola

Ah to be young!
To fly with a touch of wind
sloughing fragments
of bare skin,
yellow dust rising.

Whirling like a Dervish
in dizzy circles
at the interface
where cerulean meets gold:
the infinity of this moment
stretches beyond the horizon.

To float free without ever
touching the ground
is a dream.

La Luz Tremenda

Las hojas caen
en el suelo.
Y la gente también
caen, como nieve.
Por la muerte
descendió con la lluvia.
Se rompió el cielo con
La luz tremenda
que nos hizo ciegos.

The Terrible Light

The leaves fall
to the ground.
People as well
fall, like snow.
For death
descended with the rain.
The sky shattered with
The terrible light
that made us blind.

La Sombra de la muerte

Ya todos los días pasan sin recuerdos.
Ya no más me dicen como me decían:
Eres joven.
La ancianidad crece mientras que la juventud
se desaparece,
como el viento en los arboles
desnudos por el invierno que murmura:
Todo ha pasado.
Todo tu amor, tu vida.
Todo el corazón, el alma.
No hay más
que la sombra de la muerte.

The shadow of death

Now every day passes without memories.
Now they no longer say as they once said:
You are young.
Old age grows as youth
disappears.
Like wind in trees
left naked by winter it murmurs:
Everything has passed.
All your love, your life.
All your heart, your soul.
There is nothing left but the shadow of death.

Pensamientos

Se murió mama, y desapareció
la última conexión del pasado.

¿Ahora quien va contarnos
las historias de nuestros antepasados?

No tú mama. Tampoco papa
que ya hace cuatro años
desde su viaje al más allá.

Y de los recuerdos de que estuvimos
aburridos de escuchar tantas veces,
que pensamos que nunca vamos a olvidar,
ya están olvidados.

¿Quien puede contarnos estas historias?
¿Quien puede decirnos los nombres
de las desconocidas
en esas fotografías viejas?

Desde que se murieron nuestros padres
la conexión del pasado se ha roto.
No hay nadie que pueda repararlo.

Al igual sabemos que nuestro presente
será el pasado para nuestros hijos.

Se repite, como un círculo,
de generación tras generación.

In Melbourne - 1938

Mum and Dad at home in 1988

Mum in 1936

Thoughts

Mum died, and our ultimate connection to the past disappeared. Who now is going to recount the stories of our ancestors?

Not you Mum, Nor Dad, now four years since he travelled to the other side.

And of the memories that we were bored hearing so many times, that we thought we would never forget, are now forgotten.
Who can tell us these stories? Who can tell us the names of those unknown people in those old photographs?

Since our parents died the connection to the past has been broken. There is no one who can repair it.

Equally we know that our present will be the past for our children. It repeats like a circle, generation after generation.

Another Onslaught

Masses of black, grey swirling
clouds, pregnant
with rain and hail, surge ominously;
dark inverted waves dependant
from the underbelly of the sky.
Thudding surf smashes beaches
sucking away sand.
Suddenly violent wind lashes treetops
vacuuming up dust, dry leaves,
and pieces of discarded paper—
fragmented moments of our lives.
The air vibrates, humming
with contained electricity heralding
the relentless thrusting storm front.
Hide, but not under a tree.
Too many are split by lightning—
massive trunks, huge branches
breaking in one explosive light blinding
instant —to fall unseen, unheard in the bush.
Thunder rattles the ground, shakes bones,
pounds heads, inducing momentary migraines.
In a furious flurry of rain
Pandanus stand stiff, outlined with
scattered shafts of translucent light;
luminous green arrows quivering
ahead of roiling-black heavy cumulous,
bunching, humping monstrous
writhing heads replete with
thunder and stroboscopic flat lightning.
Gravity straining heavy air condenses water drops

into fragmented sparkles — reminiscent of
diamond earrings — that dangle from the tips
of spiky Pandanus leaves, before a renewed gust
shatters them, blasts them down to pockmark
the sand beneath. To think that in those
black anvil clouds air twists and rises
with speeds too violent to comprehend.
It travels up so fast that water frozen into
crystals of ice carried aloft ablate or
melt with friction through the air.
And once again they adhere to each other;
blobs of water lumping together, rising higher
and higher to refreeze, and roll
over the edge of the cloud mass where
gravity inexorably brings them down
as monstrous ice balls, clubs of hail
shattering tiled rooves, crushing new cars,
knocking birds out of trees, stunning them,
killing some. Inevitably, when the storm
moves out to sea where it may
metamorphose into something less dangerous,
there is a quiet moment of rejoicing.
The sun tentatively peeks through
disconnected remnants of shattered cloud.
Birds with short memories joyously take flight.
Steam rises from wet earth and warm asphalt.
Rolling invisible waves curl
up into the air to form new clouds
recycling for another onslaught.

...fragmented sparkles after rain...

Homecoming

He came home in a box,
her one and only son
who in the woods at home
could live like a fox.

He came home in a box
held high on the shoulders
of his mates who slow marched
across tarmac to a waiting hearse.

His mother cries. Tears
overwhelm her as she waits
for her son, for answers
that could allay her fears.

But all she gets are false
platitudes, crocodile tears; sad faces
that convey nothing. 'We are sorry
for your loss,' the leaders say.

'This nation mourns another son.'
And then they add, 'we pray
for him, but the fight must go on.
We cannot let evil win.'

Do you care? His mother demands.
Would you send your sons
and daughters there? To such alien lands
where only rock and sand skins the earth?

Where jagged mountains cut thin air
that is hard to breathe? How can anyone
fight and survive over there amongst
invisible enemies, ghosts that explode

and tear bodies to pieces, where even
a child can be a martyr, where love has gone
and only unbridled hate survives? What
are we doing in places like that?

Why? She implores. But there is no answer
she can hear, no words they can use
to satisfy her need to know.
All their false platitudes and sad faces

do not alter the fact that she is among
an ever-growing group of mothers and fathers,
sisters, brothers, and friends whose loved one
came home in a box.

Talk to me...

Talk to me about
something,
anything but what I don't want to hear.
Tell me about rain falling,
wind
blowing ferociously over the sea,
gentle breezes caressing soft skin,
leaves
falling, bare branches, a naked tree.
Tell me about crepuscular skies,
cloud stream wisps across a
faded stratosphere,
a new moon, a blue moon,
anything…
the smell of rain after a drought
when deserts burst into life,
of flowers' sweet perfumes,
the hum of bees hovering in search
of nectar.

Talk to me about
miniscule insects floating in the shade
of a tree, the slither and rustle of snakes
and lizards in bush and grass,
red wine in fine glass,
afternoon coffee at a sidewalk café
oblivious to the world around us,
sumptuous dinners and old cognac.

Talk to me about
our childhood, playing games
in the street until dark
with the first stars glittering in an arc
across a black sky,
our imagination,
our creativity before television
distracted our course. The thrills we had,
the good times… even the bad.
Tell me of the sea, a fine beach, soft sand
between our toes, and the icy touch
of salt water on the first day
of summer, when gulls squawked,
wings fluttering
to keep them in place as they squabble
over discarded pieces of food.
Grass stretching to the horizon, pollen
making eyes and nose water, trees, rainforests,
desert dust storms…

Talk about all that, and more,
but do not talk about what I don't want to hear,
for that will come soon enough.

Llorando

Abre las cortinas y descubrí
Que el mundo estaba llorando con mí
por mi preciosa Moniquita ya no está, se murió.

Aunque tengo nuestro hijo en casa, siento
tanta soledad que a veces pienso
que no puedo seguir, pero la vida sigue.
Mi Moniquita fue a mi lado por cincuenta
años, pero ya no está. Hay un hoyo en mi corazón
de tanta inmensidad que no puedo llenarlo.

¿Qué voy a hacer sin ella?
La vida que ahora tengo que vivir parece
incomprehensible.

Cada vez que miro donde Moniquita estaba sentada
por la ventana en su asiento, en su espacio favorito
y no la veo, empiezo de llorar.
Mis lagrimas se caen como la lluvia afuera.
Pienso que ella está llorando conmigo
aunque ya no más puedo verla.

30-9-2021... Four days after Monica passed away. It was raining outside, and very cold. I sat by the window staring at the rain and thinking of my beautiful Monica and how I would never see her again, except in my memories, and felt compelled to scribble the above poem in Spanish in my notebook. I never gave it a title then, but **LLorando** *(Crying) seems appropriate.*

Talk to me *I wrote 10 years earlier when Monica had a severe allergic reaction to a medication prescribed to her and ended up spending a week in hospital when she came close to dying. It gave us one hell of a fright.*

Some thoughts...

I know little of modern poetry,
blank verse – it seems to me –
is designed to obfuscate,
to confuse, distract, to negate
logical thought by using obscure
analogies and discordant metaphors.
No longer is there metre and rhyme
which to create takes too much time.
In this world, music is made by machines,
or computers programmed with memes.
Visual images flash and change with
enough speed to induce epileptic fits
while bombarding us with sound bytes:
sub-aural thumps that vibrate bones,
rattle marrow, shake brains into jelly.
With exhortations everywhere to constantly
consume, is it any wonder poetry that rhymes
seems out of place – from other times?

Those who live in large cities – and more
of us do every day – forget that a leisurely
life is a better way, that constant activity
wears a body, ruins joints, creates ulcers,
worry lines, headaches, falling hair,
and a life exacerbated by hypertension,
allergies to poisonous air, and frustration
with the inability to achieve a desired
outcome. We drown ourselves with
a cacophony of noise, and kaleidoscopic
images that brainwash us day and night
with no obvious outcome in sight.

Conurbations of large cities
are like clusters of galaxies.
Hundreds of millions of people
linked by complex patterns of roads
that resemble a massive circulatory system
are not unlike the billions of stars
circulating within each of the galaxies
that rotate around others in clusters
tied together by unseen dark forces
and gravity. Some, over billions of years
crash into each other while stars are devoured
by black holes.

Cities, with centres becoming black holes,
uninhabitable spaces, dangerous places,
while outskirts expand, are not unlike galactic clusters.
Will they slow-crash into each other with
catastrophic annihilation? Is it possible? Few
will accept this premise of a future demise.
Perhaps modern poetry with its blank verse,
its non-rhyming lines, reflects an urban curse
and our unwillingness to attempt a simpler
less complex way of life. What we
should remember is the land will survive,
and even if we don't, Earth will always abide.

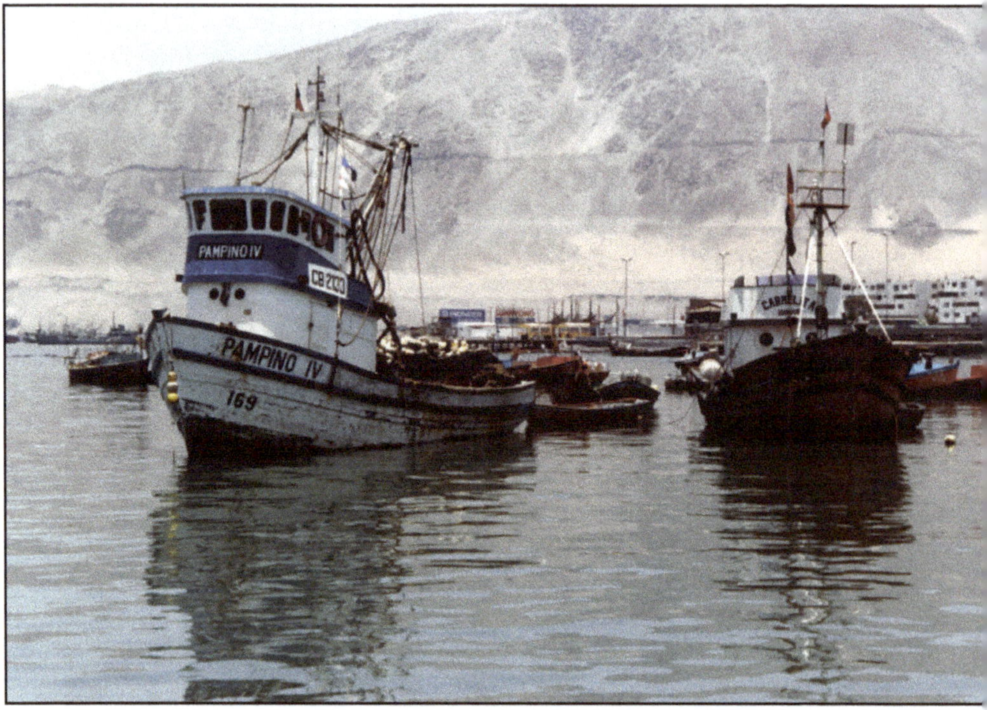
PAMPINO IV
PAMPINO IV
169

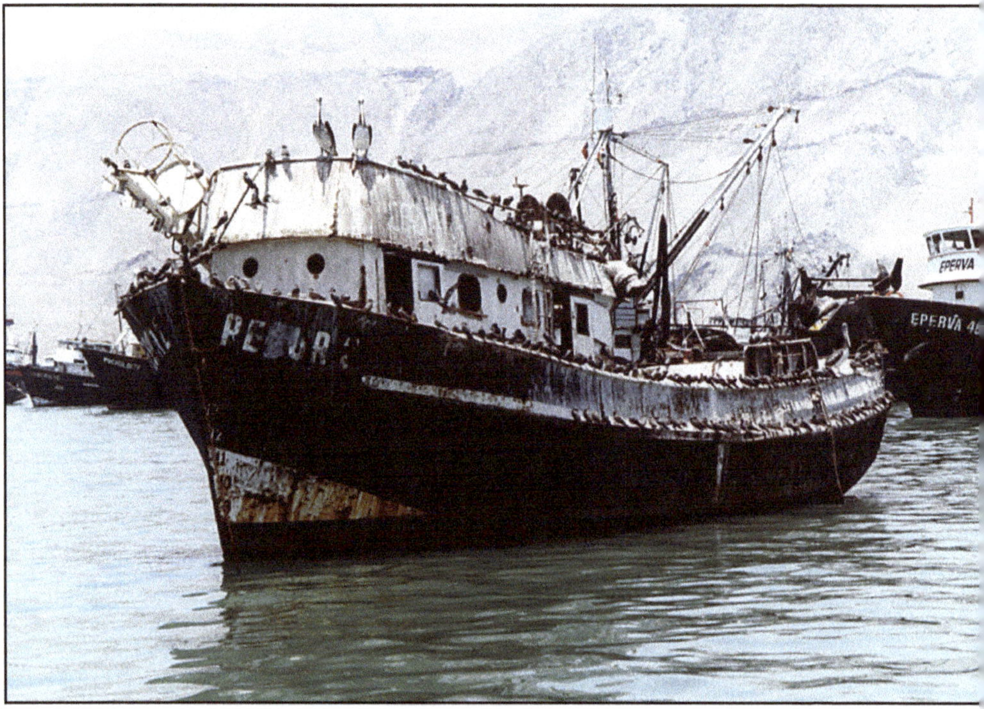
EPERVA

Leaving Iquique.

Leaving Iquique,
with the foul stench of sardines
processed into fish meal
that permeates everything,
where gruff winds from the pacific
rub against towering grey ramparts,
the jagged edges of the Atacama,
the bus grinds up a narrow street.
Hardly fleet, it pushes cautiously
through heavy air.

Behind us, tangled electric wires
vibrate in clusters atop lamp posts,
dust devils whirl along thin streets,
vultures blurt and fart in tree tops
surrounding the central plaza.
Dirty beaches edge a bay filled
with rusting fleets of abandoned trawlers,
hundreds anchored in lines to wait
the return of the Humbolt with its lost
sardine schools.

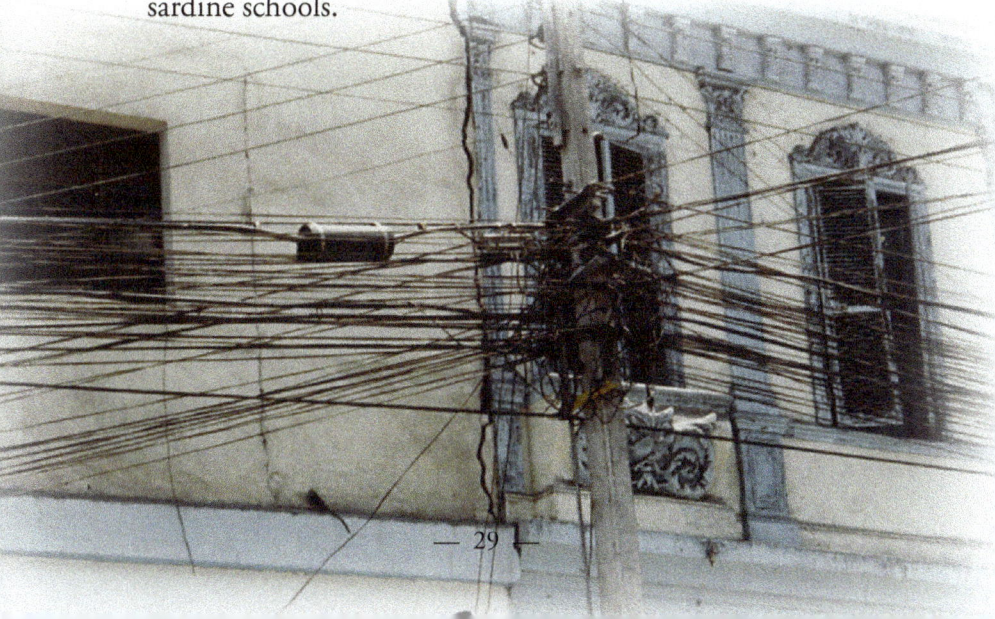

Sea lions sprawl on black rocks
barking at tourist boats that come too close.
Forlorn, hungry perhaps, for they also
miss the sardines. Dry heat makes them lazy
so periodically they drop into the dark sea
to cool off and search near-empty waters.
The processing plant is silent, but
the stench still emanating from it
blankets and suffocates Iquique.
There is no escaping it other than to leave.

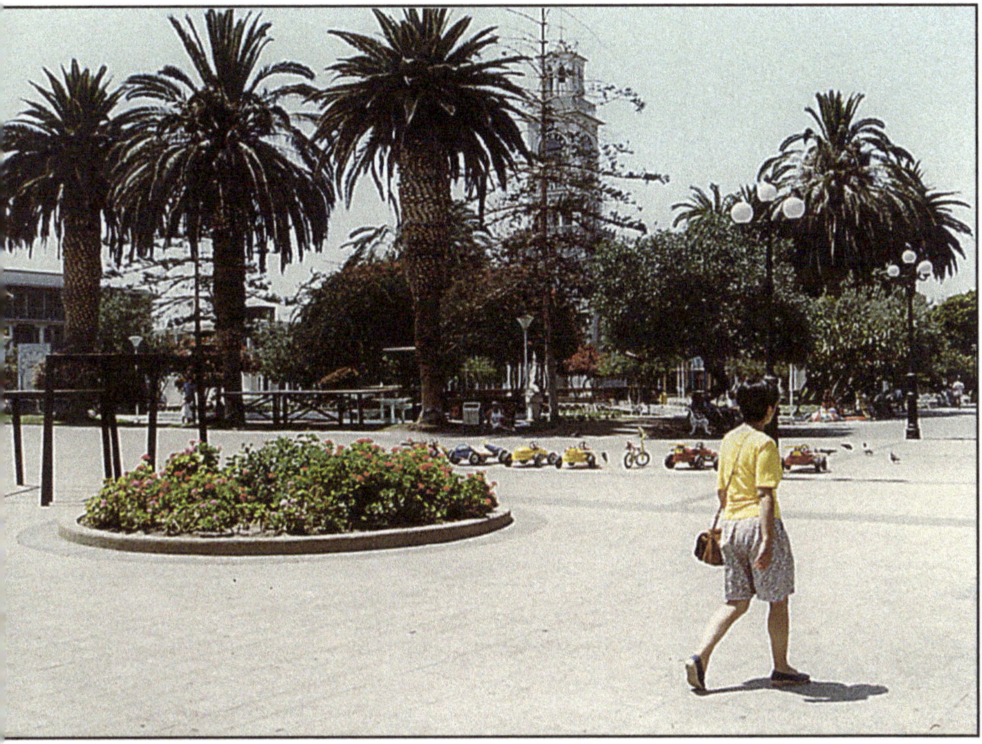

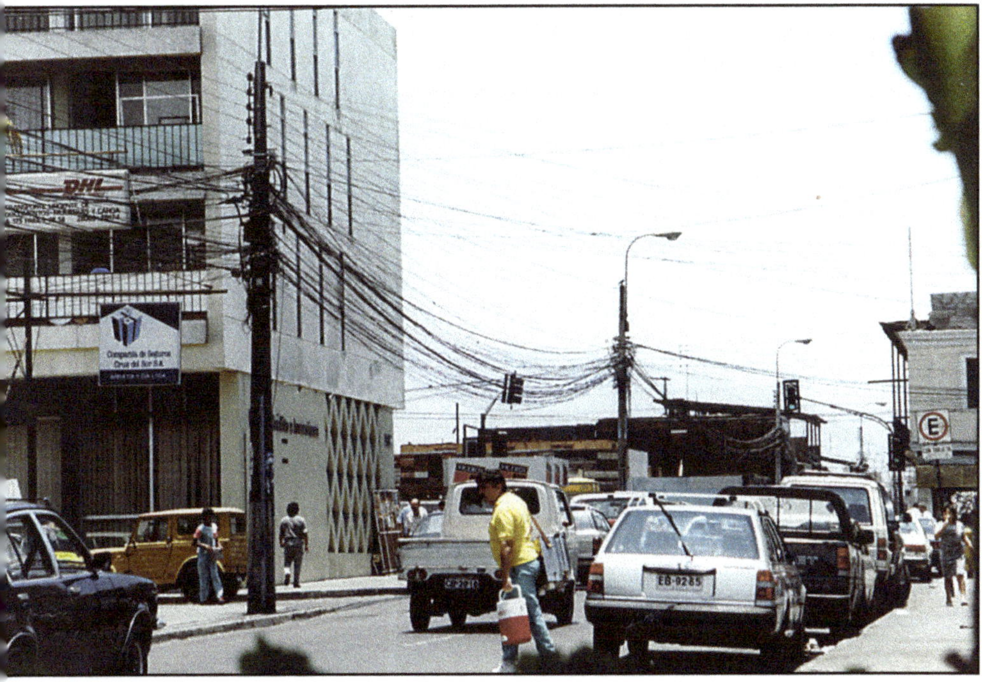
DHL
EB-9285

The bus moves with grinding gears, and
spurts a fog of noxious carbon monoxide.
It turns right at the top of a long rise, around
cracked adobe walls splashed with flaking
faded paint bleached by the intensity of the sun.
It never rains at the edge of the Atacama.
Holding a crumbling curtain to one side,
a tiny young girl peers out through
a grimy ground-floor window.
Does she see the slow passing bus?

The height of her window is the same as
the equally dirty windows of the old bus.
Catching a glimpse of her tiny face
as the bus slows to edge
cautiously around the building, I wonder:
Is her face one of despair or one of Hope?
It appears blank, but in that moment
that I see her something shows
while the bus shudders into the narrow turn,
gears grinding, black fumes spewing.

A child's face in a window… blank…
Schrodinger's cat. Alive or dead? Open the box.
The face shows nothing, and everything at once…
boredom, patience, hope, curiosity, despair;
it's all there, but it doesn't exist until I choose…
What is it I see? Her eyes follow mine
for less than a second, yet locked together
for an eternity. The bus turns,
the window is gone, the face lost,
left behind with the rest of that dusty town.

The bus continues its laboured climb
towards grey ramparts that hide barren
emptiness where nothing wants to live,
not even insects or a blade of grass.
A hint of copper glistens on pebbles, but
the enervating greyness of the Atacama
overwhelms all as it pushes down
from The Andes, threatening to bury
this cluttered moribund town on the edge
of the deep blue Pacific.

Of all the things I saw in Iquique,
the momentary glimpse
of that child's face in the window
has stayed in my mind.
The rest has vanished.
In such a brief glance,
I saw so much potential,
so many divergent possibilities,
that I can't help but wonder,
what has become of that child?

Our garden is a bit on the wild side, unkempt, but it has its own beauty, and it does attract other creatures...

Refuge...

There is a place where over time
palms and golden canes grow huge
with tree ferns in shadows sublime.
Our garden, our backyard is a refuge

attracting insects that hover and shimmer,
buzz, whir and crackle, while birds flit
through branches, singing with abandon,
searching for places to nest.

There are bright flowers, and
sweet nectar for hovering honey-eaters,
and ants that farm with aphids
leaving sticky trails along thin stalks.

With infinite textures and shades
of green, each frond, each leaf, each plant
is a unique expression of nature's beauty.
Lorikeets attack the fruit of an umbrella

tree, squealing with delight, reeling
in swooping arcs, crawling along slender
pendant flower stems picking at sticky
sweet seeds, wings of iridescent green,

exposing yellow bellies and purple heads
in contrast to the sombre black and white
of butcher birds and magpies. Black crows
have their own sedate beauty as they search

The wattle was full of bees gathering nectar...

for pestiferous cockroaches, for nuts
and berries. Crows and magpies
even eat the flesh of fallen mangoes
after fruit bats at night while gorging

cause heavier fruit to drop to the ground.
We had a baby water dragon once
that claimed the area around the pool as
its own. It ran incredibly fast

with its head held high, chasing insects.
It sat immobile to survey the pool surrounds,
a stone extrusion on mossy rocks. But after
watching it grow for a year it vanished,

never to be seen again. Was that
kookaburra which sometimes perched on the pool
fence complicit in its disappearance?
Was that raucous laughter a sign of

contentment after a good feed?
But there are other lizards, tiny, dark things
which dash furiously everywhere, and geckos
that race up windows, walls, under eaves upside down

chasing bugs, silverfish and mosquitoes.
Often at night after rain tiny green tree frogs appear
as if by magic, hopping with soft sloppy sounds
as they jump from leaf to ground to window.

There are toads too — ugly poisonous
unwanted pests that invade with alien
desires. Nothing touches them. Their poison
will even kill a snake if it eats them.

There was a goanna once, one night.
I thought it was a fallen branch on the path
and bent to pick it up to throw away,
when suddenly it rose up, head swinging from side

to side and ran straight at me. It made me jump,
heart aflutter because it was almost a metre
long. It must have come from the nearby bush
reserve, a small wilderness in an urban sprawl.

Sometimes we are visited by two ducks
that float placidly in our pool, and one day
a strange shape at the bottom turned out to be
a wayward turtle, that had wandered out

of the reserve at night, and lost along dry streets it
found the smell of water in our pool irresistible. We
rescued it, returned it to the lake in the nearby
reserve. It ran excitedly across the lily pads

and disappeared into the murky water.
We didn't know turtles could run so fast.
I let the garden grow wild, as nature intended
so other creatures will find it, as I do, a refuge.

Flores

Llega la primavera y el jardín de repente
está lleno de flores, los árboles también.
Sus bellísimas colores atraen pájaros
que cantan lindas melodías, llenando el aire
con sus sonidos ricos,
e insectos que vengan para alimentarse
con néctar, y con sus vuelos y movimientos
volando aquí y allá, andan fertilizando las frutas
que mas tarde van a aparecer.
Infelizmente la primavera no dura
mucho aquí, y muy luego llega el calor del verano
y todo el jardín cambia con altas temperaturas
y vientos calientes, pero hay flores en el verano también
aunque son diferentes de las de la primavera.
Y así el jardín tiene otro tipo de belleza.
Solamente en el invierno está el lugar
poco desnuda cuando las hojas de los árboles se caen
en el suelo para proteger la tierra abajo y
dejar nutrición en preparación para la primavera
que llegara, como siempre.

Birds in our garden...

An early morning visitor...
A pink Galah looking in the grass for wild flowers gone to seed.

Some of the birds in our garden.

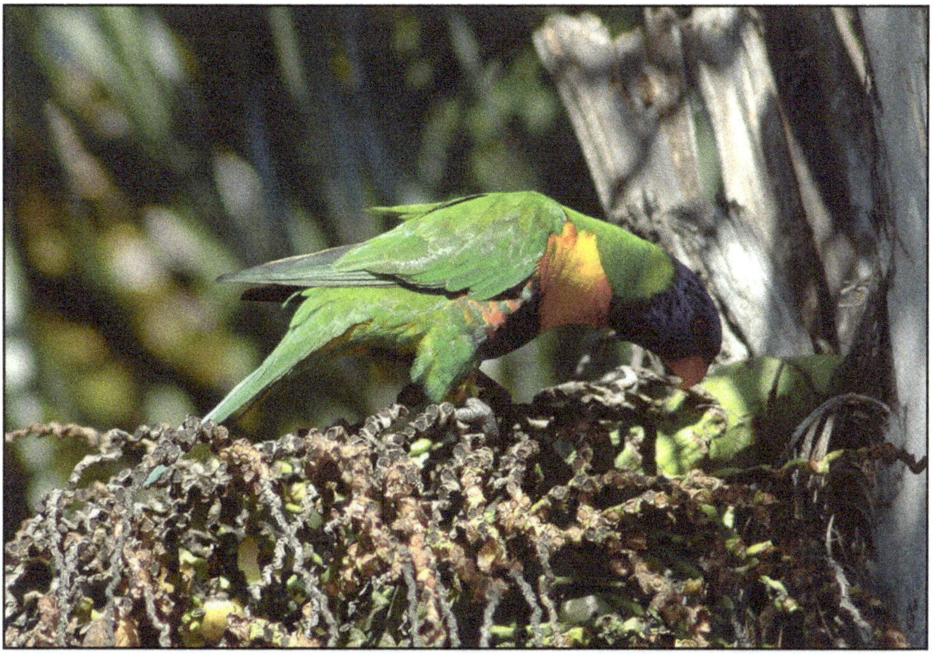

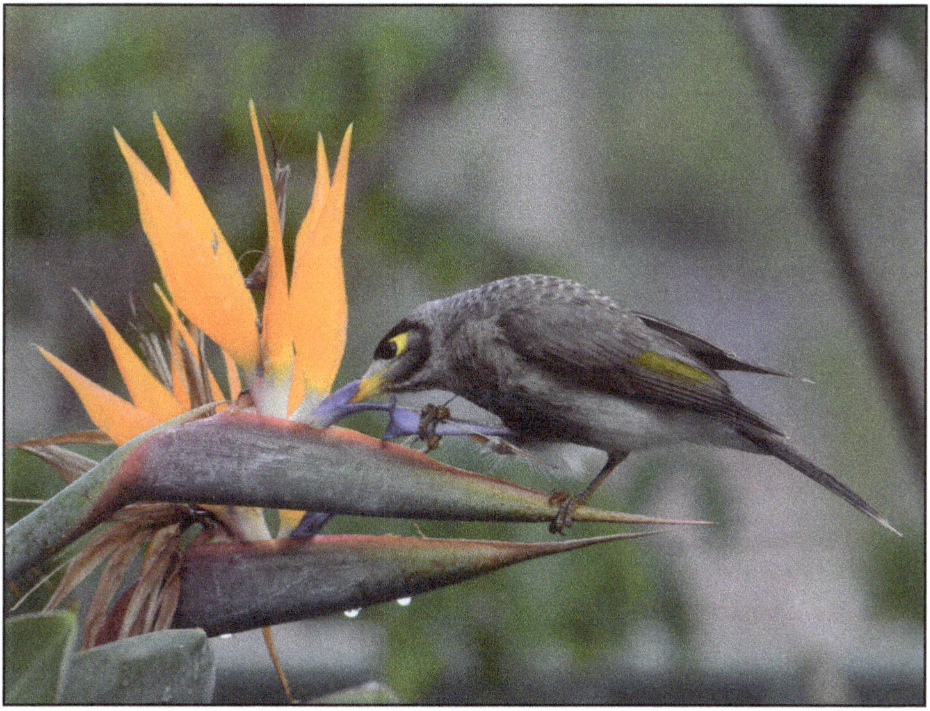

Every spring, baby pigeons, crows, and magpies feel safe in the garden.

Even a bush turkey found refuge in our wild yard after bush fires devastated its habitat at nearby Burleigh Heads Bluff.

The pool is not only there for the birds.

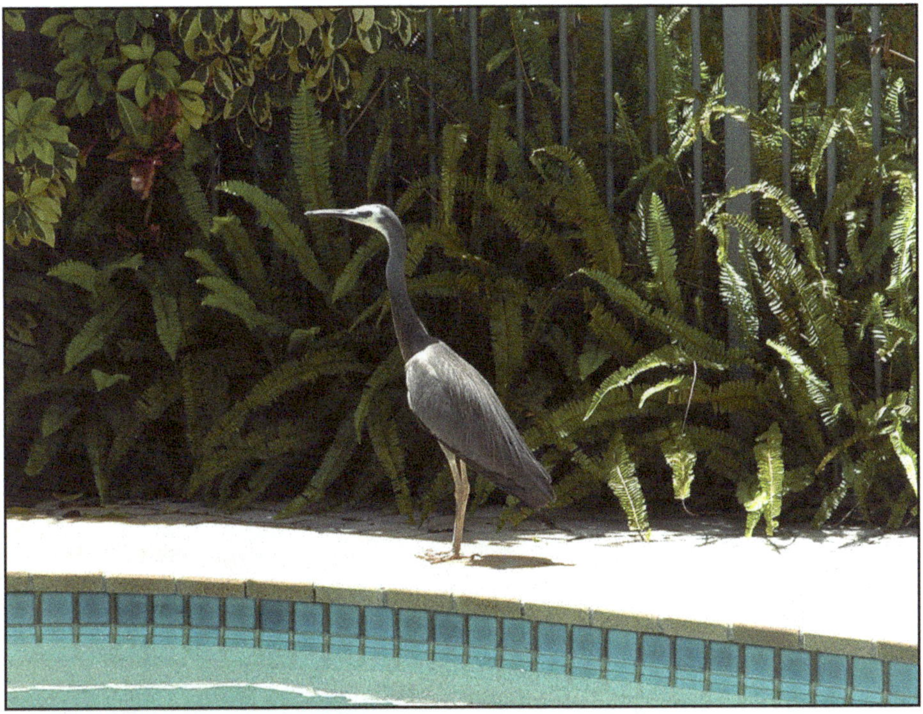

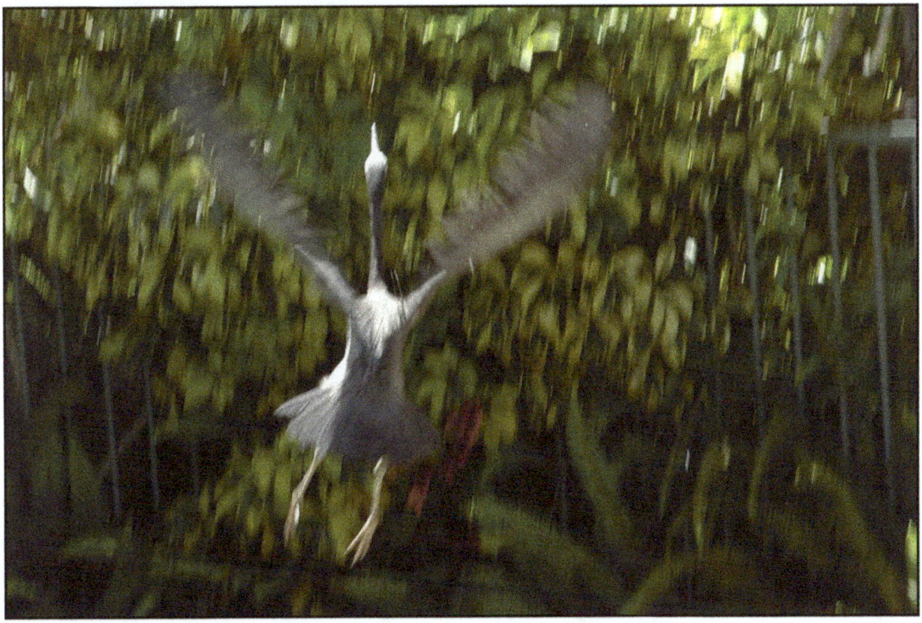

A duck in the pool

One morning in September I went into the yard and saw I a small duck swimming in our pool.

This was not unusual in itself because we often had a duck or two spend an hour or so in the pool on many different days over the years. You sometimes see them in pairs foraging on people's front lawns in the winter after a cold night when dew covers the grass making it damp forcing small insects and worms to emerge.

The lake at the Robina Woods golf course where there is an abundance water bird life is not that far away from us, perhaps half a kilometre.

But this time it was unusual because the duck was there every morning when I went into the yard. As soon as I got near the edge of the pool the duck would swim to the furthest part from me.

Soon after leaving the pool, the duck jumped up onto the edging and quickly slipped under the overhanging leaves of the Golden Canes planted by the pool's edge. I thought this was unusual because other times, the duck would simply fly away after a short time in the pool.

The next morning, looking through the window I saw the duck again on the edging and it took off and flew up over the house, so I went outside and had a look under the cane fronds and there was a nest.

There were seven eggs in the nest.

It was almost impossible to see her under the dried palm fronds as she sits on the eggs in the nest. Her colouring blended perfectly into the background.

About an hour later saw the duck returned. She landed in the middle of the pool, swam to the edge beneath the Golden Canes and hopped up and quickly slipped in under cover and could no longer be seen.

She stayed there all day. If I went out early enough I would see her swimming in the pool for a few moments before taking off and flying away. She would return about an hour later, to the pool, to her nest where she would stay unless I went too close. If I got close she would jump into the pool and swim as far away as she could in order to distract me.

Searching online I discovered it takes about 28 days for ducks to hatch and so we waited, and watched. The weather after the second week started to get very hot and by the end of the third week, we were every day with temperatures in the mid-30s C. It even got to 35 C one day, and all that time the duck sat quietly on the nest.

In fact, 2019 was the hottest year on record.

After 28 days I figured the eggs must have been affected by the extreme heat. It was unusually hot for late Spring. As we edged into December and the beginning of summer, the hot weather continued without relief. Too bloody hot. I thought for sure the eggs had been killed by the heat, and the poor duck would be sitting there starving while she waited for them to hatch.

When five and a half weeks had gone since I first saw the eggs in the nest I was positive the ducks were not going to hatch. I didn't know how long the eggs had been in the nest before I actually saw them, so five and half weeks at the least seemed too long.

A couple of days later (*December 13th*) I opened the bedroom curtains. The sun had been up for at least an hour and a half even though it was just past 6-30 am and immediately looking at the pool I saw the duck standing on the pool edge and unbelievably there were the 7 ducklings in the water directly beneath her struggling to get out.

They couldn't flap their tiny wings and jump up like she could. She jumped back into the water and swam around with the little balls of fluff trailing along behind. She jumped out again and they struggled to do the same but the height from the water to the pool edging was too high.

They had probably followed her into the water at dawn just after they had hatched. They looked as if they were exhausted. I tried to catch them and take them out of the water but they kept swimming away so I couldn't get near them from the edge.

The mother got back into the water and swam as far away from me as she could get with the little ones following close behind.

The mother duck was becoming agitated so I had to figure something out. They needed some kind of ramp for them to walk up to get out of the water. A wooden plank was no good because it floated and kept moving as the water rippled. Suddenly I thought of a rock bank. Make a ramp out of rocks in the water so they could walk up them. I grabbed three large sandstone rocks from the garden and placed them in the shallow end to create a rough ramp. The rocks were half submerged with just the tops sloping up towards the rim of the pool.

While I was doing this the duck and her 7 babies were swimming back and forth as far away from me as possible. Walking around the pool towards them I managed to make them swim towards the rock ramp. The mother jumped out a metre before it and the little ones bunched up underneath but couldn't get up. As I walked nearer, she edged along away from me and stopped just beyond the rock ramp.

The little ducklings swimming along trying to keep up with her bumped into the rocks and immediately started climbing up them and out of the water. As soon as they were out of the water, they followed their mother back to the safety of the nest under the Golden Canes. There they stayed for about two hours.

While downloading the photos I had taken into the computer, a movement outside caught my eye. The ducklings were following their mother around the side of the house.

Grabbing the camera, I ran after them. They went along the west side until they got to the gate which was closed and couldn't get out. They ran back along the side of the house as I approached and I followed them as they went to the back of the yard.

   The mother was searching for a way out.
   Eventually they returned to the pool and after staying in there for a few minutes climbed out over the rock pile and went back to their hidden nest. I opened both side gates, hoping that they would find their way out and down to the nearby lake in the golf course where there are plenty of ducks, other water birds, turtles, fish, frogs, and many other native creatures.

Back into the pool where for a while they felt safe…

I had to go and do some shopping, and when I came back at four-thirty I checked the nest and it was empty. There were several crows flying or hanging around the Golden Canes, and I thought something awful could have happened. Those crows would dive on the ducklings and eat them without compunction.

There were no ducklings in the nest and the mother was nowhere to be seen. There was no way she would desert them. She would fight the crows to protect her young.

I couldn't see them anywhere in the yard so I assumed they must have found their way out and were heading down towards the lake in the park beside the golf course. I was disappointed in not being there to see them leave. I would certainly have followed them at a discrete distance to make sure they got to the lake safely. Unfortunately, there was no way I could know which way they went.

The next day I went down to the nearby lake to see if I could see the duck family but had no luck.

It's a huge lake and the only part I can access is inside a public park. The lake extends into the Robina Woods golf course and makes a wide circle a through the golf course so the ducks could be anywhere in there. I did see several ducks in amongst water hens, ibis, and other black looking ducks with a white beak.

No sign of any ducklings so our little family did not come down to this part of the lake. I hope they are okay. But then this happens somewhere around here every year and there are always plenty of ducks so I suppose they will survive.

Four months later - April 3 - 2020

I Heard a splash in the pool and looking out the window saw two ducks had landed in the water and were swimming about.

One of them jumped up onto the coping and spent awhile examining the place where the nest with the ducklings had been a few months earlier. I suspected it was the same female duck that had laid the eggs. The other duck kept swimming around while keeping close to the spot where the female was looking carefully beneath the palm fronds. Eventually the larger, I presume, male duck jumped out of the water and onto the coping to stand next to the female. A few minutes later they dropped back into the pool and swam around for a few minutes. Then suddenly, as if startled, they leapt up into the air and flew off in a north westerly direction.

Was the duck examining the empty nest to see if it was still a safe place to lay more eggs in the future? Or was she showing her companion (life partner) where she had nested?

Am I anthropomorphizing by assuming more intelligence than basic instinct? Were they looking for a safe place or reconfirming that our yard and swimming pool is a safe location for nesting in the future? Will they come back periodically to check again?

I can only wait and see.

Having satisfied themselves that it was a safe place perhaps to nest again in the future, they took off. I'm sure they will be back.

Noises in the night

Every time we hear a possum at night
it gives Monica a fright. She's the nervous type
who jumps at every unexpected sound.
When we hear the sudden flutter of tiny
footsteps followed by a loud thump,
I know a possum made a jump
from the higher part of the roof to the lower edge
where a short leap across to a tree or a palm
will give it access to developing fruit,
a clump of berries, or new leaf shoots
that it can devour with relish.
Every time I try to grow tomatoes,
the plants never get more than a few centimetres tall
before a possum strips off the leaves
and the plants wither and die within days.
The cherry tomatoes, which would be better
for it to eat, never develop. It doesn't touch the
tarragon, basil, or parsley: too aromatic perhaps?
We used to hear the possums raucously
serenading each other in the mango tree
at the back of the house. Always in the middle
of the night they would wake us up with their hissing
and coughing, sounding like some monster from
a horror film. If you didn't know that awful noise
came from a possum you would be frightened.
I took a photo one night as it sat on the pool fence
outside our bedroom's sliding glass door.

There it was, sitting on the pool fence after running across our bedroom roof and jumping into the mini phoenix palm at 2 am.

Usually the possums were gone by the morning, but one night we had a storm and one stayed in the tree out front, and was there all day.

We used to be invaded in the summer by
flying foxes or fruit bats when we had the
mango tree growing. They would flap over the roof,
and hang upside down in the tree squabbling over the fruit.
As soon as twilight deepened, they came in swarms.
Partially eaten fruit would drop to the ground, left there
for the crows and other smaller birds and insects
to devour in the morning as the sun came up.
The mango tree got too big and we had to get rid of it
because its roots stared undermining the foundations.
At twenty metres tall and loaded with fruit,
there was too much to eat, and with the bats feasting
it became too messy and smelly, and noisy to keep.
The neighbours cut down their palm trees as well.
With those gone, the fruit bats no longer came at night,
to everyone's relief and delight.
Nobody wanted the fruit bats.
Unfortunately, the lorikeets also stopped coming since there
was also nothing left for them to eat.

Food for the possums and the birds.

Sands of Time

From the highest tide mark to the sea's
lowest ebb, cool water-sculpted ripples
of hard sand tempt bare feet.
Running, flying over wet corrugations; our
semi naked bodies brushed with salt breezes
disturb the work of nature.
Incoming tides barely affect the hard ripples; soft,
winds fill our footprints with talcum-fine sand.

Can we leave footprints in the sands of time?
There are dinosaur footprints frozen, in stone
that was millions of years ago the mud of a lake-bed.
Will some future being find our footprints
in this shoreline's ripples, or will they be washed
away, forever lost? Humans are but passing creatures
in a long line descending from ancient mists
and strange things that lived momentary lives.

Who are we to expect to leave a record in
the long years that lie before this planet's end?
Will future beings ponder the traces humans
left in the ripples of time? Will they wonder
why our existence on this world was so brief?
Will they think we had abandoned our world?
How can we be certain our cities of concrete, stone,
steel and glass will stand the onslaught of time?

Humans are arrogant to think Time will not take
their cities and grind them into dust to be transported
by wind and water, carried by rivers to the sea where
continental shelves accept infinitely slow deposits.
Will far future palaeontologists decipher

our existence from the detritus of our lives?
Our works are no more than sighs lost in a gentle breeze.
They are as sand rolled into ripples by the action of seas

at the interface between water and land.
We inherited a world that was beautiful and
perfect for life as we know it. How could we have
changed it to make it so inimical? Long after
we are gone it will be for other stranger beings
to make of this world what they can,
to wonder over remnants left by those long gone;
our existence ephemeral, but everlasting as ripples in sand.

Sand in an hourglass

The immutability of time
restricts our lives to a finite line.
There is no going beyond the end,
no comprehension of before the beginning,
little understanding of the time between.

Fragments; obscure moments,
good, bad, indifferent, jumbled together,
are confusing when young,
inexplicable or forgotten with age.

Like grains of sand in an hourglass,
our moments cascade over each other
until all that is left is emptiness,
and apprehension of what may be
beyond our end of time.

Every life lived is nothing more than
a fractional moment of eternity…
each of us less than a single grain
of sand in an hourglass.

Questions...

Geoglyphs and petroglyphs and ancient paintings in caves tens of thousands of years old — are they no more than the ancient equivalent of modern day Graffiti?

Do we need to explain their existence with profound theories of how ancient people communicated with each other, with disparate visitors and unknown tribes through the use of visual messages?

Could these cave paintings, as profound and beautiful as they are, the vast complex designs of stone Geoglyphs on mountain sides, the intricate carvings in rock petroglyphs that were created in ancient times, be nothing more than a simple statement to affirm that in that place at that time, the person or the people who made those things existed?

Could they simply be territorial markings? Is it too simple an answer for us to accept, so we imbue them with layers of deeper meaning? Or are they the beginnings of human language expressed in visual terms between peoples who spoke vastly different dialects?

Did they really mean to tell stories and histories, or is that what we would like to believe?

John Litchen

Is Graffiti today a means of communication? Or is it the marking of territory? …A statement saying this is my place, respect it or keep out? Is it like a dog pissing against a lamp post, a cat spraying a wall?

Why do people paint their names on large rock outcrops along the road sides, scrawl their names in public places, and spray-paint blank walls, trains and other utilities? Could it simply be that they want it known for all time that they existed, that they were individuals who lived and were more than simply one among thousands and millions of other unknown beings?

Above: Easter Island geoglyph. Below: Petroglyphs in the Atacama Desert.

Is their desire to do this no more different than the people who made those ancient prehistoric cave paintings, created giant Geoglyphs, carved petroglyphs?

Can we not accept graffiti as art just as we accept that those ancient prehistoric artefacts are art? Is it because the medium is different? Is it because the location is different? What will people in a thousand years think — assuming the spray-painted graffiti still exists — when they see these markings in abandoned urban environments?

Will they look at it as we look today at those other ancient art forms? What really is the difference?

Graffiti in San Francisco circa 1990.

JOY IT FOR
AT IT IS. DONT
RRY ABOUT WHAT
SAYS.
QUEST

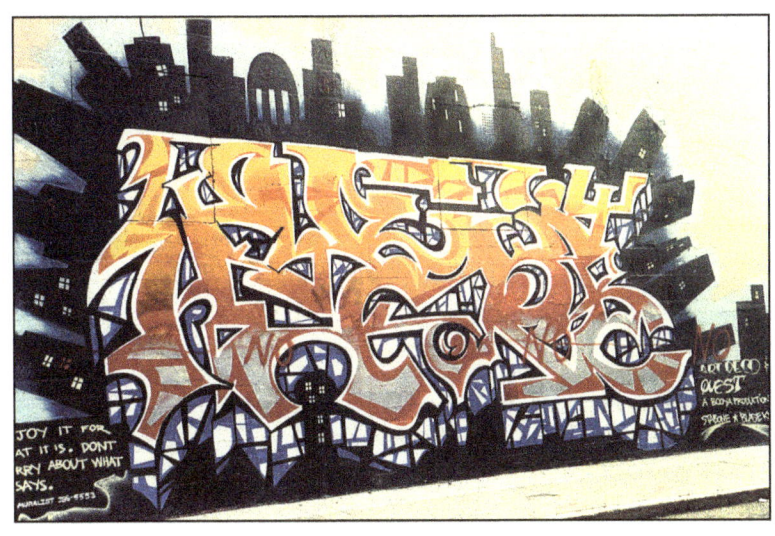

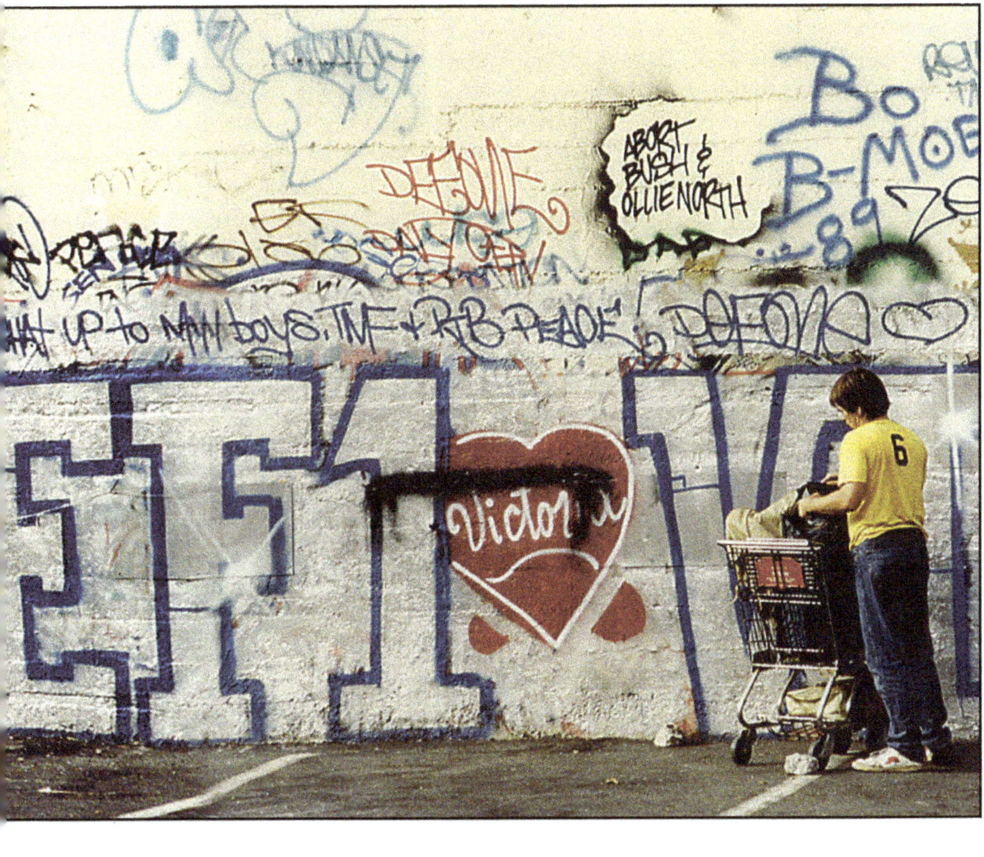
ABORT BUSH & OLLIE NORTH
Bo
B-MOB
89
Victoria

The Gellibrand Pile Light

Originally it had been a light tower on a floating base,
a lightship anchored in place.
Sometimes during severe storms it would break free
and float down the channel out to sea, which confused ships'
navigators who used, and needed the light to see
where the rocks off Point Gellibrand and the back-beach
reached the edge of the channel.
Eventually a series of pylons were driven into the sea bed
and a lighthouse was built on top.
The light-keepers lived out there, beneath their light
which they maintained within clear sight,
of the channel for ships to avoid the reefs and rocks
extending around and out from Point Gellibrand.

We loved that lighthouse and used to swim out
to snorkel and skin dive beneath its pylons
where sting rays and fish lived in comparative safety.
There were muscles and cockles on the rocks beneath
and on the pylons holding up the structure. Schools
of fingerlings and shrimps filled the water with sparkles
of light refracted off their tiny bodies darting around.
Fishermen often came out at night to catch a bonanza,
while drinking beer as they recounted fish tales.
During the day it was a sight to behold as it stood proudly
declaring it was safe to pass by here as long as you stayed
on its seaward side.
When heavy fogs blocked vision of the channel,

the surrounding sea and land, a foghorn loud enough to
vibrate the bones of anyone walking along the foreshore
filled the blankness with mournful wails, but even so,
a ship blinded by the fog sometimes came close enough to
scrape against the pylons. It happened enough times
to discourage people from living there, so it was abandoned,
its light left to operate automatically.
It began to fall into disrepair.
Then one foggy night in 1976, a large ship crashed into its base
and did so much damage the Port Authorities declared it unsafe,
too expensive to repair.
The bastards set fire to it,
burnt it down to the waterline. And that was it.
The lighthouse was no more, gone forever.

The sea beyond seemed so empty without its light
shining the way for incoming ships.

The gift of sight

Life— all of it as we know it on this lonely planet,
has some way of perceiving light, an organ, some form
of an eye, multiples of eyes, even some feeling in the skin
which perceives the difference between dark and bright
that can translate reflected wavelengths of light
into images the brain conceptualizes
as solid and real… as something three dimensional
separated from its surroundings.
Sight— is something each of us takes for granted
until it becomes blurred, begins to fade, produces
multiple astigmatic images which no amount of squinting
can overcome. And when peripheral vision begins to fade
into the dark edges of tunnel vision, it's too late for anything
to be done. No more driving at night, it's too hard to see.
Only is daytime light strong enough to hold
at bay, the dark tunnel.
Light— which we need to make sense of our world
is also that which destroys our ability to perceive it,
taking away our perception of beauty by capping eyes with
white circles of cataracts, causing cancers that destroy
the iris, making the macula degenerate… and what can we
do about it? Bit by bit, parts begin to malfunction as we age,
skin dries and wrinkles, bladders weaken, hearts become erratic,
breath falters, but worst of all we have trouble with our eyes.
Glasses— at first seem to be the solution. Once again
we can see clearly with sharp images delineated,
but not for long. Soon, changing vision demands new lenses,
new frames, and even with these reading becomes a chore
instead of a pleasure. Books pile up and now most of them
are never going to be read. They will gather dust because it puts
too much strain on the eyes to read them.
It's better to sit quietly in an unfocussed garden
to enjoy warm sunshine and fresh air.

John Litchen

En La Playa

La primera vez que caminé en la playa,
para decir lo menos, fue extraño.
No pude entender como la superficie no
fue sólido, tampoco líquido, pero algo
en el medio que rasca mis pies.

La arena también fue muy caliente,
y levanté mis pies rápidamente
para atravesarlo, para entrar el mar
donde podía usar el frio del agua para quitar
la sensación que mis pies están quemando.

*Eso fue una memoria de mi niñez
que tuve después de un sueño.*

Muy luego me acostumbre, porque
anduvimos muchas veces a lugares y playas
en diferentes regiones costeras
que me gustaban mucho. Como adulto, con mi familia
muchas veces anduvimos a estas regiones recordados,

para caminar, y gozar el aire fresco
que no existe en la ciudad donde vivimos,
para ver como el mar cambia la tierra cuando toca
suavemente la arena, o con la ferocidad de tormentas
con vientos fuertes, y olas tremendas esculpiendo

las rocas, y sacando arena para dejarla en otras partes;
Eso siempre me gustó. Y ahora, aunque estoy viejo
todavía me gusta caminar cerca de la costa o en la playa
si pudiera, porque siempre recuerdo con placer
estos primeros veces que caminé en la playa.

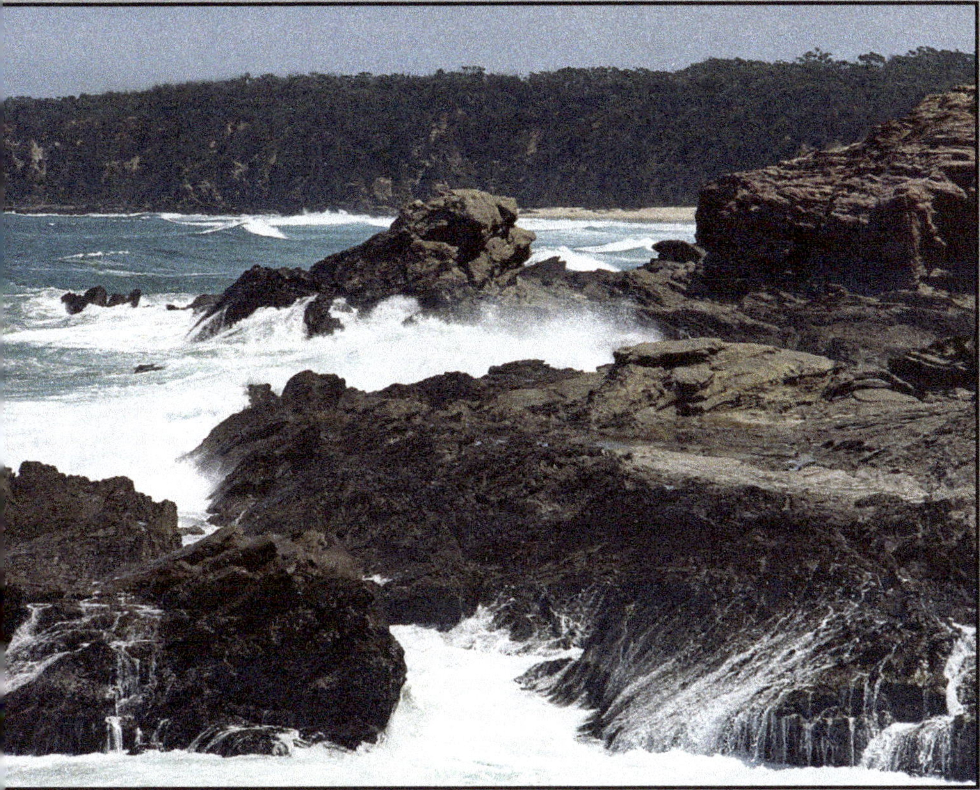

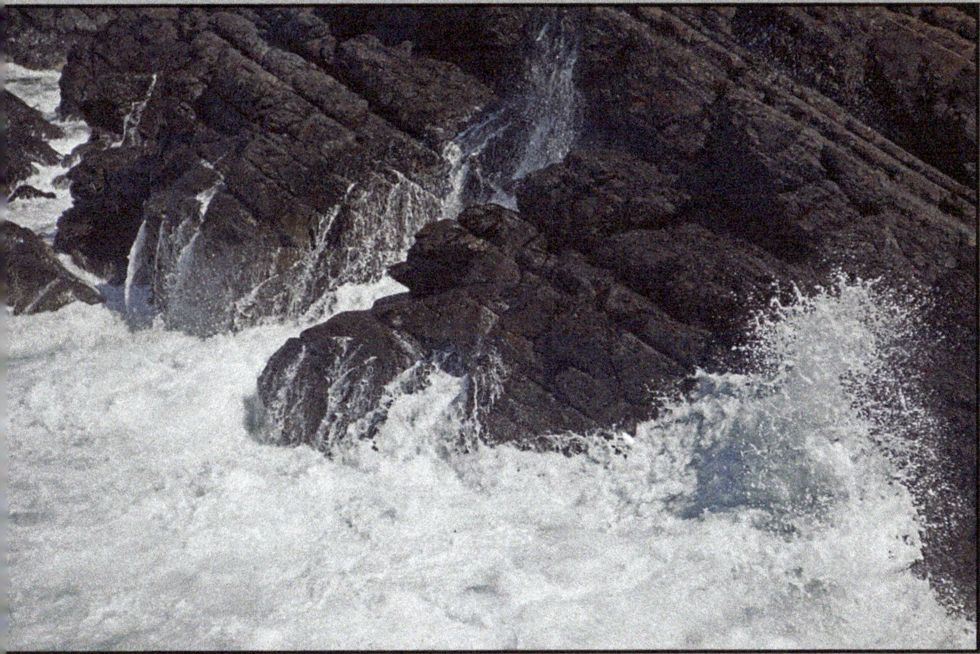

Empty Eyes

Her blank face has eyes of glass staring into space.
What do they see, the future, the past?
Gusts of wind ruffle her hair
swirling around where she sits as immobile as stone;
marble the colour of bone.

With the house behind her obliterated, only its foundation
tells them what was once there.
Pieces of human remains, scattered and singed among ashes
attract vultures and black crows which
scatter with raucous protests as we approach.
Smoke drifting up from charred wood is
snatched by restive winds and a brisk breeze
before it can bruise the sky.
A tiny ash covered body lies on its side, a frieze
carved from strange wood, beside a scorched cradle.

'Come on, we can't stay here,' one of them says.
'There is nothing we can do.'
They walk around her, careful not to disturb her view.
'She's already dead.' A small trickle of blood
down the side of her face has dried a dark crusted red.
They leave the woman, and tramp
across flat rice fields still damp after the water has
been drained off, ready for harvest.
'There's a storm coming,' one says and points
to black clouds billowing on the horizon.

'We need to find shelter fast.'
Leaving the dead woman remembering the past
they struggle through the unharvested rice, churning paddies
to mush, exhorting each other to hurry before the storm hits.
They slog towards distant hills.

The Path into Darkness

The valley of lost rice fields now days behind them,
with the thought of that woman's empty eyes
reminding them of what they were running from,
they enter a long narrow pass with jagged rocks,
and slippery stone walls cutting like a razor slash
through seemingly impenetrable mountains.
They fight for balance on a high narrow path.

Their backs pressed hard against the sheer rock wall,
with toes overhanging the edge of the precipice below,
they shuffle sideways, not looking down for fear of falling.
First moving one foot, heel hard against the rock,
until it finds a stable spot, and then shifting weight
the other foot moves to the place vacated by the first.
With extreme caution, they inch along.

This so-called pass is nothing more than a tear
in the mountain. The walls of bare rock rise
above until they disappear into dark roiling clouds leaking
moisture which dribbles down the sheer sides of the chasm.
Slimy moss grows with slippery abandon and they must be careful
not to slip as they shuffle along slower than snails.
Far below a dirty stream tears along the bottom of the chasm

leaping over fallen rocks, roaring like a waterfall, creating wet
sound waves that rise up enveloping them with mist.
They drag their backpacks, their guns, their meagre supplies
along beside them, for to carry them as they did in the fields
of abandoned rice way below and days behind
would unbalance them, and they would topple into the chasm.
"Are you sure we're going the right way?" one of them mutters.

"Not even a mountain goat could negotiate this…"
"The old man said it was narrow…" the leader reminds them.
"How much narrower can it get? We're already moving sideways."
"We can't go back…" and the implication
of what would happen if they did is left unspoken.
They shuffle a few more sideways steps. Dislodged stones
cascade into the stream far below, the sound of their falling

submerged into the noise of the water tearing along the chasm.
Catching his breath, the leader takes more sliding sideways steps
edging around a slight bulge, and the others follow.
From a distance they would seem like ants crawling along
a thin line etched diagonally into the sheer wall of the split mountain.
From further away they would be completely invisible
against the magnitude of the jagged peaks lost in the clouds above.

"No one would ever come up here," the second in the line says.
"Precisely," the leader responds. And a moment later he says,
"There are rocks in those clouds. No one in their right mind
will fly through them. They have to go over the top."
"And that's too high for anyone to see us…"
"Will you arseholes stop talking and keep moving," the last man
in the line grumbles. "My legs ache too much to stand still."

Making sure his head is pressed firmly against the rock behind,
the leader glances down to see how much of his feet
are actually on the narrow ledge. Only his heels and instep
are on the ledge. His toes look over the edge into empty space.
Shit, he thinks, if it gets any narrower, we are all fucked.
Don't think about that. Stop looking down. Keep moving.
Somewhere up ahead is the cave, and

the slit in the side of the rock opening into a tunnel
that passes under the mountain. It has to be there.
Looking ahead to see where the path leads,
he notices with dismay that it stops hard against a wide
extrusion of rock that juts out over the edge of the chasm.
Fuck! There is no way around that.
He stops shuffling and stares ahead.

The old man was wrong.
"What's up?" the man behind him asks.
"A fucking dead end…"
"I can't see from here…"
The leader shuffles further along allowing
the second man room to edge around the curve
so he too can see.

"I might as well jump off the edge and
be done with it," the leader mumbles.
"Didn't the old man say we had to make
sure we went right to the end?"
The leader glances back at the second man who adds
to his question. "Go right to the end…only then will you see it.
That's what he said wasn't it?"

The leader says nothing, too weary to respond.
"You'd better be right" the second man adds. An empty threat.
Ignoring him the leader resumes his slow sliding shuffle
along the sheer wall. The others like zombies follow.
"There's nothing there," a hollow voice utters with despair.
Another has come around the bend and can see the path's end.
"Keep moving," the leader calls back to encourage them.

Finally, the leader reaches the end.
Hidden behind the first part of the bulge
jutting out over the chasm with the raging waters below,
he sees a narrow cleft barely wide enough to allow
a person of his heft to pass through.
"It's here," he calls out. His legs quiver with small spasms.
"Just like the old man said," he reminds them.

He stares at the narrow slit in the rock face.
"You can only see it when you are in front of it."
He eases into the gap, bending his knees so his head will pass,
and pushing his gear in front he squeezes cautiously in.
Inside the gap he discovers it becomes wider
the deeper he goes. He shoves his gear aside
to make room for the man following.

"I won't fit," the second man says.
But he has no choice. He can't go back.
The others behind won't allow a retreat. He must
squeeze through the cleft or the others behind
will be unable to enter. He pushes his gear in and lowering himself,
he exhales so his chest collapses, forcing him to become thinner.
The rough stone scrapes against his chest and back.

He fights the urge to breathe so he won't become stuck.
From the darkness inside the leader reaches out,
takes the second man's arm, pulling him forward.
The man groans as a jagged rock cuts a line along his ribs.
The leader lets go and moves further into the darkness.
Once inside the second man takes a deep breath;
turns and assists the next by dragging his equipment in

allowing space for him to squeeze through the slender gap.
Each in turn does the same for the man behind
until all are enveloped in the darkness of the cave.
The little light that penetrates the slit of an entrance
barely illuminates more than the first few metres.
Beyond that the darkness is impenetrable.
They sit exhausted, legs quivering, breathing harshly

while they recover the energy lost on the long shuffle
against the chasm wall. Suddenly, outside of the cave
they hear the screech of air vehicles screaming up the valley
searching for them. Can the entrance be seen from the air?
Or will they fly past too fast to see the narrow slit in the rock
that hides them? The scream of the passing air vehicles
and the hissing of displaced air makes them shiver.

If it had taken any longer to traverse the long narrow ledge
they would have been spotted and vaporized,
wiped out like you wipe out a line of ants crawling up a wall.
But for the moment they are safe… if that actually means anything.
The old man had told him of how they came through the tunnel
from the other side, from the high hidden valley
only to discover no way down.

They had carved and chipped the narrow path with axes and adzes
so they could get down through the chasm (Unbelievable!)
to the rich valley below where they settled and lived
an abundantly rich and well-fed life until the invaders came.
"They killed everyone," the old man had told him;
"everyone, with their weird lights and strange radiations.
You must get up to the hidden valley, find them, kill them."

And he told them of the path and the cave
and the tunnel through the mountain. But where had the old man
and his people come from in the first place?
There must be another way in and out. They had to get
into this hidden valley from somewhere else.
That's what we need to find, that other way out.
When everyone has sufficiently recovered from their ordeal

the leader takes his torch and lights the path ahead.
"That's the way," he says pointlessly because they know
they have no other choice but to go on.
Standing up he hefts his backpack up over his shoulders.
With his torch spreading a feeble light he knows won't last,
he moves forward into the deep interior of the cave.
The others grumble as they follow the path into darkness.

It takes days before they emerge from the darkness.
Hungry, gaunt, sweating and dirty, dark rings under their eyes,
they emerge into a feeble light, grey with shadows, a dark
penumbra reaching down from a mass of lowering cloud.
"What kind of place is this?" One of them mutters.
Fat drops of water fall down, moisture too heavy to stay
suspended in the air. Their vision of the valley ahead is obscured

by the heavy wet air, giving the appearance of being
underwater. Silvery grey waist high grass quivers,
undulating with long slow ripples.
They hear the loud hissing of rain further up the valley
beyond where they can see. There is no other sound
and their voices are muffled, dead-like without animation.
"There's something wrong with this place," the leader says.

"I don't like it one bit," the man behind him says.
As they reluctantly move forward, their steps are muffled
and they feel their feet sinking into something spongy.
Looking back, they can't see the split in the side of the mountain that is
the only path to the world outside. But they see their footprints
where the grass they stepped on is flattened.
"If we have to, we should be able to find our way back," one whispers.

"Why are you whispering?"
"I don't know…"
"Fuck, this place already gives me the shits," another mumbles.
"Forget that crap," the leader says. "We need to move forward.
We need to find water. We need to find another way out."
And without waiting for an answer, he walks into the thick grass.
His feet squelch as moisture in the ground seeps up.

Something slithers away deeper into the grass.
"Was that a snake?" the biggest of them asks.
His feet sink into the ground up to his ankles.
"I got water in my boots," he says.
"I hate fucking snakes," the leader says as he pushes onwards,
heading towards the sound of running water. "There's a creek,
or a river ahead. We should set up camp there."

"Only if there's a clearing. I don't fancy being in this long grass."
At the end of the line, the last of the seven following
in the footsteps of those in front has trouble breathing.
"Can you slow down a bit," he calls out.
The man in front of him slows down to help.
"It's like I'm trying to breathe underwater. I can't get enough air."
He stumbles as his feet stick in the mud, almost falls.

The others, unaware of the last man's struggle to breathe, push on.
Far above the clouds obscuring this hidden valley, the sun,
having gone beyond the mountain tops, throws the valley
into ever deepening shadow. The heavy cloud cover
over the hidden valley is now almost black, with no moon
or stars to lighten the darkness.
Emerging from the waist high grass, the leader stumbles over

unseen rocks. Layers of cracked basalt separate the long grass
from the running water of the creek. "This will do," he says.
"We'll set up camp here." He drops his backpack,
moves over to look at the water. There are flickers
of bioluminescence as something dark moves swiftly towards
the edge, towards him. He staggers back.
"What is it?" the big man asks.

"There's something in the water," the leader says.
"Can we find our way back to the cave if we can't stay here?"
"I took a bearing," the man behind him says. "You can't see it
from here but I can find it."
"We could follow our tracks back. That should be easy."
"I don't think so," the last man adds. "Look back there."
They turn and look.

The grass is undulating from both sides towards their trodden path.
As they watch the broken stalks swell, start standing up,
quivering as if to shake off whatever had squashed them.
Within moments there is barely an indication of the path they had
made to the flat rocky ground beside the creek. The lush grass
stands tall, shivering slightly. The undulations cease,
and all is as before; their tracks completely obliterated.

"Fuck, what is this place?"
"Is that really grass, or is it something else?"
"What else could it be?"
"I don't know, but it's not like any grass I've ever seen."
"Forget that shit," the leader says. "Set up the tents.
We'll need some cover because it will rain again."
With practiced ease they have their small tents up.

And darkness envelopes them as above
the dense cloud layers covering the valley, the sun sets.
They crawl into their tents, try to sleep,
but it evades them as slithering sounds in the
long grass sends shivers along their spines.
The total absence of light is more terrifying
than normal darkness. Specks of light flash

inside their eyes. Whispering sounds, slithering sounds echo in their ears, filling their heads with disturbing noise. Minds run rampant imagining the most horrible of creatures sliding out of the darkness, creatures that have no need to see, but go by feel, and smell, slimy things... One of them emits a gurgling scream.

All of them leap up, torches alight.
"What the fuck," one of them yells as his torch illuminates the ground outside his small tent swarming with thick, slimy black snakelike things writhing and twisting around each other as they attempt to evade the light. Some of them flop back into the unseen water, splashing as they

disappear into the blackness beyond the torchlight. One of them is missing, not standing in the group with the torches lighting a space around their tents. There is movement in the missing man's tent, muffled, gurgling sounds, slimy black things slipping out of the tent's opening. They race over, pull open the tent flap, and in the torchlight

they see their companion covered in slimy eels. Massive fucking black eels. The light makes the eels retreat so they can see the damage done to their friend. He is no longer moving. One massive eel has entered his mouth suffocating the man.
The men batter the eels, forcing them to relinquish their meal. Only the one inside the man's mouth stays

and try as they might, they cannot get a grip strong enough to pull it free. "Fuck this," the leader says. He staggers back from the tent, leaving the man and the massive eel inside. The moment they move away from the tent, other eels begin to return.
"There's nothing we can do for him."
"We can't stay here," another says, "or we're all dead"

"We've got to go... get the fuck out."
They shine their torches on the thick grass hoping to see
the path they had earlier taken, but it is gone. All the grass
is standing tall, not one blade crushed, broken, or flattened
which could have indicated their path from the tunnel
through the mountain into this valley.
"Which way do we go?"

"How the fuck would I know," the leader says. "That way."
And he points directly away from the creek that runs
beside the flat area where the tents are set up... the creek
full of predatory eels. "The sooner we leave the better."
They kick at the eels again writhing around their legs.
"Leave everything. Let's get out of here."
A look back sees swarms of eels sliding up out of the water

slithering towards the tent where their dead companion lies.
They turn and run into the long thick wet grass
which welcomes them by trying to twine around their legs.
Pushing their way through they tear the grass loose as it grips
them, not strong enough to hold them.
"Make sure you don't fall over or trip," the leader yells
as he struggles to get through the ever-thickening grass.

The further away they get from their abandoned camp
the deeper and thicker the grass becomes, and the harder
it is to push through it. It doesn't tear away from underfoot
as it did closer to the rocky escarpment by the creek.
Its roots are firmly embedded in deep soil, and they hold
well. The thicker fronds writhe and wrap around the legs
and waists of the men struggling to push through.

It impedes their movement so much that the only way
to proceed is to draw their long knives and slash it,
cutting it as they push through. A fierce loud hissing
emanates all around them. The grass writhes furiously,
oozing sticky ichor where it had been slashed. One of the men trips,
pulled over by stalks tightly wrapping around his feet.
He slashes furiously at the grass trapping him.

He yells "Don't get that sticky shit on you, it burns."
But before he can free his feet, more thick grass wraps
around his arms, his waist, his neck. "Help me," he calls,
but the others move on, not having heard him.
They hack and slice, cursing and shouting,
moving forward in the direction they hope leads
back to the crack in the mountain, their only way out.

"Maybe those fucking alien things breed up here in this
hidden valley, that's what forced the old man and his
tribe out, down onto the plains," The leader mumbles
as he hacks and saws at the writhing grass; grass that
becomes thicker, more rubbery as they cut through it.
"This isn't fucking grass," he yells out, "Its a field of tentacles.
Like a million octopuses trying to grab us."

He slashes it with more fury than ever.
It grips harder the further into it they go. But they have
no choice. They have to get back to the cave and the tunnel
they used to enter. "Come on Guys, keep moving,
Don't let this shit stop you." The others don't hear him,
too busy slashing and hacking at the writhing tentacles.
Only four of them make it back to the edge of the plain

where the rock is too hard for anything to grow on,
where they eventually find the crack in the rock wall that opens
into the cave and the tunnel through the mountain above.
Finally, they can sit and rest, wait for the sunrise
so they can see at least part of the way into the tunnel.
"I'd rather take my chances out there, where it's normal
and we can see those fucking aliens coming than

in here with those eel things and grass that isn't grass."
Sitting inside the entrance of the cave, and shivering in the cold
they wait, minds blank, struggling to process what has happened.
"Maybe it's some kind of alien nursery," the leader says at last.
"Or maybe it's those bastard's food supply," another adds.
"Who the fuck knows," the leader replies, staring into the darkness
beyond the cave entrance, waiting for something hideous to crawl in

and attack them. In their rush to escape they left everything behind.
"We can't stay here. We have to go back."
"Do you think we can go and get our stuff when it's light?"
"I'm not going back there, no fucking way." The leader is adamant.
"You can go back if you want, but I'm not. As soon as it's light enough,
I'm heading through the tunnel to the other side. I'd rather be
out there than in this shit valley where everything wants to eat you."

And they fall silent, each enveloped in their own misery.
With dawn a pale light filters into the valley outside the cave entrance.
They hear a loud humming and tentatively move towards the
opening to look outside. They see one of those alien ships
that had been hunting them, descending, drifting down from
the cloud cover above the hidden valley. It settles onto the flat rocky
ground where they had pitched their tents. Two dark, indistinct figures

float out of the ship to stand on the ground beside their tents.
"Shit, they'll come looking for us when they see the path we made."
"No they won't," the leader says. "That stuff has already regenerated.
You wouldn't know anyone had been there except that we left
our tents and backpacks by the creek."
"What if they come looking for us?"
"Hopefully they'll think we were eaten by the eels, or the grass,

whatever the fuck those things are."
More humming as another of the alien ships descends
to settle beside the one already there. Another two dark
figures emerge from beneath the second ship, and they join
the first pair in examining the tents and equipment left
beside the black creek and the monsters within it.
"I'll bet they're wondering how we got into the valley," the big man says

watching the alien figures examine their abandoned tents.
"Let's go," the leader orders and turns away from the entrance back
into the darkness of the cave. Reluctantly, the others follow.
It is a slow trek. They don't have torches this time, but as their
eyes adjust to the darkness, they see a glimmer within the rock sides,
a faint glow that allows them to see enough to move forward.
"At least we know where one of their bases is, and when we get back…"

"If we get back," one of the others qualifies.
"When we get back," the leader repeats. "We'll be able to tell
the Air-force where to drop bombs. A couple of
tactical nukes should give them something to think about."
"Wipe out the whole valley. Kill every fucking thing in it,"
the second in command says, as he remembers his mates
and the horrible death they encountered.

With that thought in mind,
they continue doggedly into the darkness
heading towards the light they know is at the other end.

A view of apocalypse

It started as an ordinary day,
driving across to South Melbourne
to buy tiles for a kitchen bench repair.
While in the store, it got darker.
and darker, but I thought nothing of it
until I emerged to discover a heavy brown
haze had come down to smother us.
It smelt dry, dusty, and gritty. It swirled and
spun and blew across the street, a series
of mini tornadoes, whirlwinds like you see
on the open plains in the west of the state.
Only here it was in the city, empowered by
fierce hot dry winds, a summer's day not
uncommon, but unusual only
because there was so much dust.

With the tiles in the boot, I headed home.
Driving along Footscray Road out of the city
I was stunned when I saw a massive
cloud of dust, a dense wall stretching up as high
as I could see rolling over everything,
coming towards me as fast as I was driving
towards it. It was rapidly dark, and foreboding
with this mass of brown dust like
cumulus clouds in a thunderstorm, rolling
relentlessly towards me, turning
day into night. It stretched from horizon
to horizon, blanketing all before it.
The cars in front had their lights on.
As they disappeared into the roiling mass
their taillights vanished in an instant.

I slowed down, an instinctive reaction
to stop by the side of the road, unsure whether I
would see anything once I was submerged in
the dust, but hardly had time to react before
it swallowed me. There was no escape.
It was frightening. Instantly everything went black.
I switched on the lights but that was as bad
as having bright lights on in a fog. I turned them off.
There wasn't much traffic at that time,
around 3:30 in the afternoon. Peak hour had
yet to come so only a few cars were immersed
in the dust cloud. Once in it, my eyes adapted
to the darkness. It wasn't too hard to see.
Visibility at street level was around 50 metres.
Fortunately, everyone had slowed down.

A massive dust storm like this rolling over Melbourne
was unprecedented. It had blown across the whole
state from the Malley, thousands of tonnes of soil
lifted up and blown away forever, blown out over
the sea, the worst dust storm in Victoria's history.
It could be seen by satellites in space.

Dancing on Sand

It got into everything even though we had
the windows at home shut. Monica saw it coming
and ran around locking every door and window.
But it still got in filling the electric power points
with dust the consistency of talcum powder,
covering the pictures, the furniture,
the clothes inside the wardrobes,
covering everything with a thin layer of dark dust
that took ages to clean and vacuum away.

We could taste it and smell it for weeks afterwards.

Seeing this massive cloud rolling ominously
towards me, and being immersed in it, made
me think: *Could it be like this at the end
of the World? Would everyone
and everything be subsumed within
massive clouds of dust and vaporized particles?
Would it be super-hot and kill in an instant like
it had millions of years ago when the dinosaurs were
wiped off the face of the Earth? And if the whole
world was covered in dust and vaporized material,
how long would it take to cool down enough for a
long winter, another ice age? Would it take days,
or weeks, years? There'd be nothing left to survive
if that happened. Humanity and every other living
thing wouldn't, but life deep in the sea might,*

*and would eventually re-inhabit the land, as it has
done time and time again.*
Pessimistic thoughts aside, inside the dust cloud
wasn't any hotter (*43 degrees C*) than it had been outside.
But that was too hot anyway.
The worst of it blew away in an hour or so, leaving
a dim haze that took longer to dissipate. The whole city,
every building and flat surface was covered in dust.
People wondered in despair how they were going
to clean up, but as it is in Melbourne, a cool change

John Litchen

blew in after the hot winds had been spent.
A slight shower washed away the worst of it.
People only then had to clean the insides of their homes,
a big enough job that seemed to take forever.

The dust was insidious, but eventually we got rid of it.
It took a lot longer to disappear out over the ocean.
From space it could be seen extending far across
The Tasman to New Zealand where it left smudgy
layers of brown on snow-capped Mountains.
The temperature that summer in February 1983 set
a new record and the drought sucked all the moisture
out of the soil leaving it so
dry and dessicated in the Malley and the Wimmera
that it was easy for the fierce hot winds to lift it up to blow away.
At its height over the city the dust cloud towered over 300 metres.
In the centre of the city traffic came to a standstill
and people breathed through handkerchiefs over their mouthes,
or found refuge indoors where not so much dust penetrated.
It was a day I would always remember.

Dancing on Sand

*But the dust storm was a warning of something worse to come.
Eight days later, still in the midst of the worst drought
ever to hit Victoria, we had a true apocalypse:
The Ash Wednesday fires.
Up to that time, the worst bush fires to ever hit Australia.
So many lives lost, so many homes, so much destruction,
whole towns turned into charcoal and ash, a warning to all of us
that we need to change, to rethink how we live
in this beautiful but fragile world
or one day it will turn on us and destroy us.*

John Litchen

Several years after we'd moved to the Gold Coast in Queensland, we woke up one morning to find the whole city enveloped in a red dust haze. A dust storm had blown in overnight, bringing the red dust of far west Queensland to smother the coast. It too blew out to sea as the morning progressed. But it was nothing like the dust storm that hit Melbourne back in February 1983. It was more like a dense fog, a brown haze that dissipated after a few hours.

Momentos efímeros

La vida está llena
de momentos efímeros
y tendríamos que gozarlos
en el momento en que existen,
porque si los dejamos pasar
estarán perdidos por siempre.
Nunca podemos volver
para recogerlos.

Ephemeral moments

Life is full
of ephemeral moments
and we should enjoy them
in the moment they exist
because if we let them pass by
they will be lost forever.
We can never go back to
capture them.

A conversation on a summer's day

"If I decide to run away,
if I decide to do that,
I won't hesitate"

"Do what you like," Mum says,
"It's such a glorious day
who wants to stay inside?

"Go ride your bike. Enjoy the day.
Who knows how long this good
weather will stay?

"Go on then, go out and play."
"Well…" I start to say.
"You don't really want to run away, do you?"

"No, it was just something to say."
"Off with you then, but don't be late.
Dinner is at eight."

A pesar de todo

A pesar de todo
siempre tengo la esperanza que el mundo se mejorará.
Pero, como la mayoría de la gente creen,
sé que la verdad es lo contrario. Se empeorará,
y así no hacen nada. Andan pensando ¿Qué podemos
hacer individualmente para cambiarlo?
Nada, es la respuesta más común.
Y por eso, alrededor del mundo nadie hace
ninguna acción para mejorar el lugar donde vive.
Pero, es un concepto falso de pensar así.

Cada uno puede hacer algo, aunque pequeño.
Millones de acciones pequeñas alrededor del mundo
añadir para mejorar el ambiente poco a poco.
Si suficiente gente empieza de pensar así,
ellos van a empezar el proceso de mejorar este mundo.
Va a tomar tiempo para ser notable, pero si lo hacemos,
eventualmente el mundo se mejorará.
Tenemos que empezar ahora.
Tenemos que pensar en nuestros hijos
y que tipo de mundo queremos dejar para ellos.

Nosotros seres humanos tenemos la culpa
por lo que está pasando, por tantas acciones
explotaciones que están envenenando el aire que respiramos,
envenenando el mar con plásticos usadas una vez, con
acidificación por un exceso de carbón dióxido
en la atmosfera, haciendo hoyos en el nivel
de ozone, calentando la temperatura alrededor,
matando tantas especies de plantas y animales
en la tierra y debajo del mar sin pensar
en las consecuencias… adiós a las peces. ¿Como podemos
continuar así antes que encontramos el momento irreversible?

Despite everything

Despite everything
I always have the hope that the world will improve.
But most people believe
the truth is the opposite. It will get worse
and so, they do nothing. They walk around wondering
individually, what can we do to change it?
Nothing is the most common answer. And for that reason,
all around the world, no one does anything
that might improve where they live.
But to think that way is false.

Everyone can do something no matter how small.
Millions of tiny actions all around the world
will add up to change the environment bit by bit.
If enough people start to think this way
they will begin the process of improving this world.
It will take time to be noticeable, but if we do it
the world will improve.
We must start now. We must think of our children
and what kind of world we will leave for them.

As human beings, we are to blame
for what is happening, for so many actions
and exploitation that poisons the air we breathe,
poisons the sea with plastic things used only once,
with acidification, with excess carbon dioxide in the atmosphere, creating holes in the ozone layer,
raising the temperature everywhere,
killing so many species of plants and animals on land
and beneath the sea without thinking of the consequences…
goodbye fish life. How can we continue like this
before we encounter an irreversible moment?

Si no cambiamos colectivamente como pensamos, será
demasiado tarde y tendremos que sufrir lo que esta inevitable,
La muerte de nuestro planeta.
Claro, que esto ha pasado cinco veces antes, y el mundo
cada vez ha recuperado, con explosiones de vidas nuevas,
y climas mejores hasta la última vez cuando apareció los seres
humanos, pero mira lo que estamos haciendo.
Sera la primera vez que una especia solo tiene la capaz de destruir
su propio planeta, y las consecuencias va a estar terminal para
nosotros y todas las otras vidas que coexisten con nosotros.
Mirando adelante, nuestro futuro parece algo malísimo.

Tal vez este mundo estará mejor sin la existencia de nosotros
humanos, y hay muchas posibilidades que va a estar así.
Pero no debe estar así.
Siempre tengo la esperanza que rectificaremos
la situación en que estamos ahora,
y en el futuro la herencia de nuestros hijos
va a estar un mundo en que pueden vivir
sin los problemas de hoy,
un mundo llena de vida con un clima amable.
A pesar de todo, esto es mi esperanza.

If we don't collectively change how we think it will be too late
and we will suffer what is inevitable:
the death of our planet.
Clearly this has happened five times before, and each time
our planet has recovered with explosions of new life
and better climates, until the last time when human beings
appeared, but look at what we are doing.
We are the first and only species that has the capacity
to destroy its own planet, and the consequences will be
terminal for us, and every other living thing that co-exists with us.
Looking forward, our future seems very bad.

Perhaps the world will be better without our existence,
and there are many indications it is going to be exactly like that.
But it doesn't have to be.
I always hope that we will rectify
the situation we find ourselves in
and that the inheritance we leave our children
will be a world in which they can live
without the problems of today;
a world full of life with an equable climate.
Despite everything, that's my hope.

Algo indisputable

Lentamente el desierto
central de este país está ganando
territorio, cada día, cada mes, cada año.
Mas gente que nunca están buscando
a donde pueden vivir acerca de la costa,
abandonando lugares más adentro

por el calor que no pueden aguantar más.
Si el mundo sigue con temperaturas
calentándose más y más, este país,
e igualmente todos los países en el mundo,
luego empezaran de ser inhabitables
no solamente por los seres humanos,

pero también para las plantas, los animales,
los insectos, los pájaros, y todas las criaturas
del aire y debajo del mar que conocimos ahora,
y también los que tenemos de conocer o descubrir,
todos estarán destruidos por culpa de nosotros.
Creo que eso está indisputable.

Ya no tenemos derechos de castigar a ninguna.
Ya es demasiado tarde por eso,
y demasiado tarde para cambiar el camino
que colectivamente hemos elegido de tomar.
Ya hemos pasado este punto.
Tenemos que existir como podemos mientras

que el mundo empieza de cambiar su clima
en la era antropogénico que nosotros ha criado.
No sabemos si podríamos sobrevivir para
conocer nuestro futuro, pero lo que se por
seguro es que ya no podemos hacer mas que esperar
la muerte del mundo que hemos conocido.

Something indisputable

Ever so slowly
the central desert in this country is gaining
territory, every day, every month, every year.
More people than ever are searching
for a place to live near the coast
abandoning places further inland

for the heat they can no longer stand.
If the world continues with temperatures
rising more and more, this country,
and equally every country in the world
soon will be uninhabitable
not only for human beings,

but as well for the plants, the animals,
the insects, the birds, and every creature
in the air and beneath the sea which we know,
as well as those we have yet to know or discover,
all will be destroyed, because of our fault.
I believe this is indisputable.

We no longer have the right to blame anyone.
It's far too late for that,
and far too late to change the path
we have chosen to take.
We have already passed this point.
We must exist how we can while

the world begins to change its climate
in the anthropogenic era that we have created.
We don't know if we will survive to see our future
but what I do know for certain is we can do nothing
more than wait for the death of the world we have known.

Addendum

Regarding the poems in Spanish...

It's funny how things come back. On the 15th August 1997, almost two years after we'd moved to the Gold Coast from Melbourne, I picked up an old book I hadn't looked at for years. For no reason I just pulled it off the bookshelf and feathered the pages to shake the dust off. I would do this periodically to keep the shelves clean, and sometimes to re-arrange the order of the books.
A fragment of my past fell out.

In 1968 I spent a year in Mexico, mostly living in a coastal city which had once been a fishing village, but when I got there had become more of a holiday place for well-to-do-Mexicans as well as American and European *Jet setters*. It was the '*IN* place' they all went to. People like Ava Gardner, Kirk Douglas, and Gregory Peck, to name a few, had houses built on cliffs overhanging a magnificent harbour. There were miles of beaches, pounding surf, day after day of sunshine, and people so friendly I couldn't believe it. I fell in love with the place as soon as I emerged from the plane, and instead of staying a few weeks I stayed for eleven months. I learned to speak Spanish in Acapulco.

My Spanish was only a colloquial street level form, and it didn't progress much beyond that because I was having a good time — which is better than saying I was too lazy to study the language in a more formal manner.

When I returned to Melbourne at the beginning of February 1969, I didn't want to lose the Spanish I had acquired so I searched the bookshops for books in Spanish: novels, short story collections, but found little of interest, only travel guides, and a few '*teach yourself*' books or texts designed to complement courses studied at schools.

In a foreign language bookshop I came across a book of poems by Cuban writers called **CON CUBA**, an Anthology of Cuban Poetry of the Last Sixty Years, edited by Nathaniel Tarn. The poems were in Spanish with English translations on the facing pages, so you could read them both together. This, I thought, was the way to maintain the language. Better than looking up words in a dictionary. I could read the original, then read the meaning of it in English which was not a literal translation.

I was fascinated. Spanish is such a beautiful language for poetry. The flow of the words, the structure of the sentences, the very sound of each word is poetical. In this book were poems filled with the joy and sadness of life, the excitement of living and the tragedy of death.

I thought the poems in **CON CUBA** were beautifully translated. I searched for and found other books of poetry, by Jorge Luis Borges, Pablo Neruda, and Gabriela Mistral.

What was great was these books also had the poems in their original Spanish with each accompanied by an English translation. Fantastic stuff!

In order to keep me thinking in Spanish, and you must think in a language to understand it, I decided I would try and write some poetry in Spanish. To me, at that stage, English was not the language for poetry. I had never liked poetry at school and had never bought a book of poetry in English.

I might mention I had never written a poem before either and thought the more modern way of not having rhyming lines or rhythmic patterns would be easier for me, especially since I was trying to write them in Spanish. I would keep them simple since my knowledge of Spanish is rudimentary.

I was 29 then, and my father would have been in his early seventies, just beginning to show his age. We often enjoyed a cup of Greek coffee (*Turkish coffee, but it was something the Greeks had adopted and made their own over the four hundred years they were dominated by the Ottoman Empire*) together on Sunday mornings and if the weather was nice, we would sit outside in the backyard to drink it.

Sitting with him one autumn day in 1969 with the poplar tree's leaves turning yellow and beginning to fall, I started thinking about what it would be like to be old, when most of your life would be behind instead of in front of you.

What would it be like to have forgotten your youth?

To sit there in the mild autumn sunshine, waiting for the end? What a terrible thing it would be to not be able to remember… Dad wasn't like that. He was active. He even made two trips overseas after that and didn't die for another twenty years. But a line of words, like the persistent repetitive chorus of a song, popped into my head so I wrote them down.

Ya todos los días pasan sin recuerdos…

I must have subconsciously been thinking of something I'd read by Jorge Luis Borges, or Pablo Neruda… I could hear their sonorous voices reciting their poetry.

I kept thinking about that line and a short time later, almost unconsciously, the following line popped into my head.

Ya no más me dicen como me decían: Eres Joven.

Once I had those two lines written down the rest flowed without any problems. I was feeling melancholy at the time, and this is reflected in what I finished writing.

La Sombra de la Muerte
Ya todos los días pasan sin recuerdos.
Ya no más me dicen como me decían:
Eres joven.
La ancianidad crece mientras que la juventud
se desaparece,
como el viento en los arboles
desnudos por el invierno que murmura:
Todo ha pasado.
Todo tú amor, tu vida,
todo el corazón, el alma.
No hay mas
Que la sombra de la muerte.

Shortly after that (in 1970) there was a lot about Hiroshima and Nagasaki in the media, about radiation, its effects, Atomic War, the Cuban missile crisis, and how close America and Russia had come to atomic destruction; MAD, that apt acronym of the 50's and 60's, Mutual Assured Destruction, being something everyone at the time was aware of.

I had a vision of what it must have been like for those poor unsuspecting people in Hiroshima the moment **Little Boy** (*the first atomic* *bomb ever used during a war)* exploded 1800 feet up in the sky above. I was inspired to write another short poem:

La Luz Tremenda.
Las hojas caen
en el suelo.
Y la gente también
caen, como nieve.
Por la muerte
descendió con la lluvia.
Se rompió el cielo:
La luz tremenda
que nos hizo ciegos.

Not long after that (in Sept 1971) I met Monica, who was Chilean, and Spanish was her native language, and with whom it was love at first sight. There was no need to write poems in Spanish as we could converse in that language together. We often switched from one language to another, since I needed to keep up the Spanish I had learned, and she needed to improve her English. She read books in English and only ever read the odd book in Spanish that her brother sent to her from time to time. He was an author and a journalist back in Santiago, Chile.

I didn't write another poem in Spanish for another twenty years until shortly after my mother died— on the 5th September 1991, and that was **Pensamientos**. It seemed right for me to write it in Spanish.

Flores was inspired by an exercise to write a poem about flowers. The exercise was supposed to be in English but I decided it sounded better if it was in Spanish, so again, another attempt to maintain the little I know about that language.

In 1970 I met editor and fellow science fiction fan John Bangsund who published a fanzine called **Philosophical Gas**. When he found out Monica's brother was the first Chilean writer of science fiction, apart from being a journalist for the magazine **Ercilla**, he asked me to write a piece about him. He gave me a copy of a Spanish SF magazine called **Nueva Dimension**, in which entire issue featured the short stories of *Hugo Correa*, the Chilean SF writer. (*Monica's brother.*)

I wrote the piece, and he published it in his fanzine, and for this issue he renamed it *Gas Filosófico*.

He gave me a copy of the issue as it was to be published, but for some reason, that issue was never actually published as he had intended, and what he had compiled for that issue was subsequently put into a later issue. I had also given him the two poems in Spanish I had written before meeting Monica and he published them as well; not in the original *Gas Filosófico* but in a later issue (#25) which reverted to its English name *Philosophical Gas*. He lost the article I wrote about Monica's brother Hugo, although it did appear in the aborted issue #21 of which he gave me a copy. He must have lost his copy of that as well because the article did appear in it. He apologised for losing it and published the two poems along with the cover below.

The cartoon character is John Bangsund, (drawn by himself) asking the seated Mexican— "What's this place called? "Where is the toilet?" and the answer from the Mexican "Who knows?"—from a guide book of Spanish supposedly written by Isaac Asimov the famous SF author who wrote over 500 books on every subject under the sun, apart from his SF novels. He never wrote such a book, that's part of the joke.

I had completely forgotten about those two poems until after Mum died and I wrote **Pensamientos**, which was published in *Tirra Lirra Literary Quarterly*, a magazine edited, and published by Eva Windisch.

I Looked for those earlier two poems but couldn't find them anywhere, nor could I find my copy of **Gas Filosófico**.

Things disappear over the years, even when you think you have put them away somewhere safe. You think you know where they are but sometimes you can never find them again. It's even more likely to happen when you move house, or interstate as we did in 1995. Then, one day in 1997 (*as mentioned*) I was rearranging the books in the shelves in my study and happened to take out a copy of **CON CUBA**. Rifling through the pages two pieces of old yellowed typewritten paper fell out, and there were the two missing poems.

I raced into the lounge and showed them to Monica. "What do you think?" I asked her.

She read them, and said, "They're very sad."

I had to agree.

They were written almost thirty years earlier and it was hard for me to imagine that other person that was me then. At that time, two years after we moved to Queensland, I was 57 years old. It's even harder for me to imagine now that I am 84 years old. I sent them to Eva Windisch and she loved them and published them in her magazine, *Tirra Lirra*. She told me some of her younger readers felt very sad when they read my English translation of them aloud, so I must have done something right.

The Spanish poems were thought of and written in Spanish first, only afterwards did I translate them into English.

Bailando en la arena (*Dancing on Sand*), I wrote after looking through old photos and discovering several faded pictures of my brother Phillip and my two sisters, Zara and Christine, from a trip we made to Cape Schanck one winter's day in 1970.

I remembered how cold it was with an icy wind coming off Bass Strait, and we all wore heavy jackets. We were on a diving trip. The sand was hard, and the girls were joking that *it was hard enough to dance on* and my brother Phillip challenged them to do so.

They tap danced a few steps and he joined in with them while I took the photos. I just had to write a poem about it when I saw those photos again many years later, so I did it in Spanish.

That was also the time when Zara's husband Fred whom I was teaching to scuba dive got into trouble between the bommies at Cape Schanck and had to be rescued. *A day none of us will ever forget (described in my earlier memoir Ephemeron.)*

A few other poems emerged in Spanish and English over the next couple of years but were not published. More recently, I sometimes write things, such as a poem, in Spanish so I won't forget the language because Monica is no longer with me having passed away in September 2021. By writing in Spanish I imagine she is looking over my shoulder to see what I have written, perhaps to suggest a correction or two…

The two poems on pages 106 and 110 are variations on the same theme, climate change and whether we can do anything about it.

I'm not sure they are poems, whether in Spanish or English. I know very little about poetry, so I prefer to call these crude attempts, *word-pictures*, which at least is apt. I see an image in my mind and the words just fall into place, or alternatively, I think of a line in Spanish and an image forms in my mind which reassures me that the words thought of are the ones matching the images in my mind.

Regarding the ducks…

17-9-21

The two ducks were there again this morning in the pool. One sat in the centre while the other jumped up onto the edge as I watched through the bedroom window. I had just got up and opened the curtains.

"The ducks are back," I said to Monica who was awake, but she didn't respond. The previous times she had been quite thrilled to see the ducks, and later the ducklings when they hatched.

I watched as one duck walked along the edge and disappeared under the golden cane palms where she had (*and I was presuming it was the same two ducks*) for two years previously made a nest where she laid a number of eggs which later hatched into ducklings. The first time there were seven, and the year later when they did it again, there were eleven. But it was too early in the year. I expected them in November, not September.

The ducks spent around half an hour in and by the pool before flying away. A day or so later they came back, and this time the female stayed while the other duck took off. She was going to lay eggs. I did think it was too early compared to the other two years, but it was warmer than usual for September, and maybe it's the warmth that triggers the egg laying time. I went out early the following morning and looked under the palm fronds and the duck was there. She immediately jumped into the pool and swam to the far edge, a tactic to draw my attention away from the nest. Once she was gone, I saw there were no eggs in there at that point. I left the area hoping she would relax and return to the nest.

There were lots of crows and birds that looked like crows or magpies crossed, being mostly black with patches of white underneath, and they were quite noisy early in the mornings and the evenings cawing and croaking, flitting about in the tops of the palms and the golden canes. They weren't here before. I think they moved into this older urban area because of the established trees in many gardens, since their natural habitats were being cleared to build new housing estates as Robina continued to expand. The other birds we used to see were frightened away by these rambunctious black birds that had been hanging around for almost two years now. This particular year there seemed to be a lot more of them than before.

19-9-21

A couple of days after the duck had settled into her nest, I woke to see the duck in the middle of the pool agitated and flapping her wings. One of the black and white crows or a magpie cross was 'sniffing' about the nest. It was not fooled or distracted by the duck's activities in the pool. It kept poking its head under the fronds to see into the nest. I opened the sliding door to go outside, and the crow immediately flew off to perch on top of a palm tree where it could look over the pool. After a few minutes it took off. I didn't see the duck, so I presumed it had gone back to its nest, but when I cautiously approached, it didn't dash out to distract me. It really had gone.

I looked into the nest and saw two eggs cracked open; their contents devoured.

I wondered if she would come back and start again, but it seemed unlikely because there were too many crows in the immediate area.

A week after that incident Monica had her devastating heart attack and later that same day 26-9-21 died in the hospital before an emergency stent could be placed into the artery leading to her heart.
(See: **Changing States,** *a memoir published in March 2023.)*

2023.
The ducks never came back to their nest again. The crows hung around for another year but have now mostly moved on.

Five memoirs detailing our life together over 50 years:

www.ingramcontent.com/pod-product-compliance
Lightning Source LLC
Chambersburg PA
CBHW040304170426
43194CB00021B/2890